MODERN
FIGHTING AIRCRAFT
F-111

Published by Arco Publishing, Inc

New York

A Salamander Book

Published by Arco Publishing, Inc.,
215 Park Avenue South,
New York, New York 10003,
United States of America.

Library of Congress Cataloging in
Publication Data

Gunston, Bill.
  F-111.

  (Modern Fighting Aircraft; 3)
  "A Salamander Book."
  1. F-111 (Fighter Planes) I. Title II. Series
UG1242.F5G865 1983   358,4'3   83-12285
ISBN 0-668-05904-4

All correspondence should be
addressed to Salamander Books Ltd.,
Salamander House, 27 Old Gloucester
Street, London WC1N 3AF, United
Kingdom.

This book may not be sold outside the
United States of America and Canada.

Credits

Project Manager: Ray Bonds

Editor: Bernard Fitzsimons

Designers: Tony Dominy
                Rod Teasdale

Diagrams: TIGA
(© Salamander Books Ltd.)

**Three-views, cutaway drawing and
color profiles:** © Pilot Press Ltd.

Jacket: Brian Knight

Filmset by Tradespools Ltd.

Contents

Acknowledgements

The author and editor would like to
thank the public relations staff of
General Dynamics and Grumman
Aerospace for their help in providing
material for this book. In addition to the
other individuals and organizations
whose contributions of photographs are
credited elsewhere, we are particularly
grateful to Thomas B. Street, EF-111A
Deputy Program Director, and M.J.
Lancaster, of the Royal Australian Air
Force Public Relations Office. Captain
Jim Rotramel, USAF, author of the
chapter beginning on page 42, has also
provided many of the outstanding
photographs included.

Author

A former World War II RAF pilot and
flying instructor, Bill Gunston has spent
most of his working life accumulating a
wealth of information on the history of
aviation and military technology. Since
leaving the service in 1948 he has acted
as an advisor to several major aviation
companies and become one of the most
respected authors on scientific and
aviation subjects as well as a frequent
broadcaster. His numerous books
include the Salamander titles *The
Illustrated Encyclopedia of Modern
Military Aircraft* and *The Encyclopedia
of the World's Combat Aircraft.*

A regular contributor to many leading
international aviation and defence
journals, he is a former technical editor
of *Flight International* and technology
editor of *Science Journal.* Among the
many other authoritative journals for
which he has carried out assignments
are *Battle, Aeroplane Monthly, Aircraft*
(Australia), *Aviation Magazine* (France),
*Aerospace International, Aircraft
Production, Flying, World Airnews,* and
the *Journal of the Royal United Services
Institute for Defence Studies.* He is an
assistant compiler of *Jane's All the
World's Aircraft* and has contributed to
Brassey's *Annual and Defence
Yearbook, Aircraft Annual* and
Salamander's *The Soviet War Machine,
The Encyclopedia of Air Warfare* and
The US War Machine.

Color reproduction by Bantam Litho Ltd.

Printed in Belgium by Henri Proost et Cie.

Introduction

Nobody even remotely connected with aviation needs to be told that the early years of the F-111, the planned all-can-do tactical fighter for the USAF in the 1960s, were marked by the biggest row in aviation. The row was triggered by the belief that the USAF had bought "the second-best airplane at the higher price" (than its immediate rival design), but the situation was exacerbated by the prolonged efforts of the Defense Secretary to make the same basic design suit the very different needs of the US Navy. Once the F-111 was actually flying everyone wanted to look ahead to quick development and high-rate production, but this was thwarted by technical problems whose extent and scale were almost unbelievable – so that the Australians did not get the F-111s they had bought in 1963 until ten years later. Even the attempts to demonstrate the F-111's capability in action were thwarted by extraordinary combat losses which had nothing to do with the enemy.

Having painfully recapitulated all this it may sound naive or even wishful thinking to suggest that in fact the F-111 was an aircraft of very great stature and unprecedented capability, which for many years has not only more than met most of its numerical design requirements but has served as the exact model for the Sukhoi Su-24, its counterpart in the Soviet Union. Does the F-111 do a good job? Of course. Need it have had all the problems and arguments? Of course not. But wisdom after the event is not particularly valuable.

What is rather odd is, first, that the more unusual features of the F-111, notably the pivoted swing-wings which so captivated the popular media, played no part in the years of technical difficulty and political in-fighting. It was certainly wrong to ask for a long-range bomber and call it a fighter. Had this aircraft been given an 'A' (for Attack) designation, instead of 'F' (for Fighter), it is very doubtful that anyone would have tried to bulldoze through a plan for one aircraft for both the USAF and Navy.

Development

During the 1950s American design teams worked on fighters to fly at over Mach 3, with weights in the 40-ton class. Such monsters, fortunately never built, helped create a mental climate for the TFX, planned in 1960 as the US Air Force's new all-can-do multirole fighter. The Secretary for Defense said it had "the speed of a fighter, the bombload of a heavy bomber and the range of a transport". Despite the protestations of the customer – the Commanding General of TAC said "I am not going to accept any goddamned 70,000lb airplane" – the end product was a 100,000lb fighter. This caused a few headaches.

When a major air force such as the USAF organizes for the next-generation combat aircraft, it is subject to inputs and pressures which pull in different directions. It wishes the new equipment to be the best, and in particular to beat anything likely in the same timeframe by the real or potential enemy. It wants it to replace particular aircraft that are nearing the end of their first-line career. It is highly desirable to make maximum use of the latest technology, yet it wishes to use only well-tried hardware and techniques that will not cause expensive delays and price escalation. And there is a fair amount of fashion influencing the sort of aircraft the generals have in mind.

At the time of Korea they were shocked at being outflown by pilots in MiG-15s and were receptive to any manufacturer who could promise more speed and height, even if it meant carrying less fuel or weapons. But by the end of the fast-moving 1950s they had overcome this fixation on performance, and in doing so had tended to move in what now appear to have been wrong directions.

New technology was abundant. In the context of the aircraft described in this book the most important was probably the pivoted swing wing (like other technical details, this is described in the next chapter). Another was the high-compression two-spool gas turbine, with its superior fuel economy, and the turbofan engine with its much better propulsive efficiency (and, by virtue of its reduced jet velocity, dramatically diminished noise). Combining these engine advances with full augmentation promised a highly superior fighter powerplant. Other new developments included titanium alloys used in primary structure; thrust reversers able to be used in flight; thrust vectoring for jet lift and STOL or even VTOL capability; complete crew capsules able to be ejected from a doomed aircraft with the crew inside; and a positive wealth of new avionics for blind navigation, terrain-following, weapon delivery and many other duties including protection against hostile defence systems.

In 1960 it would have been possible to combine all these in such a way as to produce a fabulous multirole fighter, essentially equal to an F-15 except in one or two relatively trivial areas where the technology had not then sufficiently matured (the cockpit displays and pilot interfaces are an example). But USAF thinking in 1960 was quite different from the thinking of seven years later that produced the F-15. In 1960 the USAF was trying to steer a course between experts, not only in Britain, who proclaimed the manned fighter obsolete, and other experts who said it was vitally needed but only as a long-distance 'stand-off kill' interceptor armed with large missiles. Yet other experts pointed out the vulnerability of airfields, and urged that all future combat aircraft should be VTOLs, or at the very least V/STOLs, able to rise thunderously off the ground from a thousand isolated sites where they would be safe from the dreaded nuclear missiles.

Ground-attack requirements

Still others insisted that the main role in practice was likely to be attacks on surface targets; and here again there was sharp division of opinion between the diehards who believed in the 'nuclear tripwire' policy and the newer adherents to the 'flexible response' doctrine. The former said the new fighter only needed to carry one or two bombs and deliver them somewhere in the general area of the target, while the conventional-warfare believers demanded the ability to carry about 48 bombs and achieve a delivery accuracy of about 50 metres.

It was clear that a new USAF fighter would have to be procured, but it could have been an agile replacement for the disappointing F-104 or a stand-off killer for Air Defense Command in place of the lately terminated Mach 3 F-108 Rapier. The man who got the ball rolling was the new Commander of Tactical Air Command, General Frank F. Everest. TAC had always been very interested in the air-to-ground business, and under Everest's supervision plans were drawn up for a new fighter-bomber to replace the F-105 Thunderchief.

In fact, the F-105 had never been a true fighter at all, but rather an all-weather attack bomber with an internal bay for a nuclear weapon. In many ways it was a great aircraft, but it needed the best runways available. TAC had made a study of F-105 operations, especially in Europe, which showed that, as the available runway length was reduced below 10,000ft (3,000m), so did the incidence of overruns and barrier crashes increase. Everest's predecessor, Otto P. Weyland, had written a detailed analysis of future TAC missions and equipment needs, and Everest was determined to get new hardware into the inventory as soon as possible.

Above: Not a 'bit more poke' but the container for the anti-spin chute on the 4th RDT&E prototype. Note the streamlined fairings outboard of the engine nozzles.

Below: From the top of a hangar at Fort Worth a photographer records the pre-rollout preparations, with technicians preparing the prototype under the scrutiny of a camera crew.

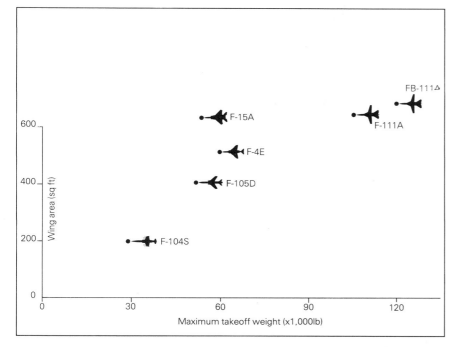

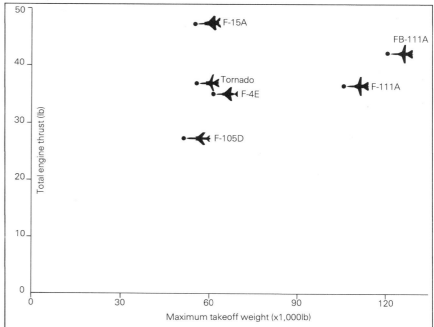

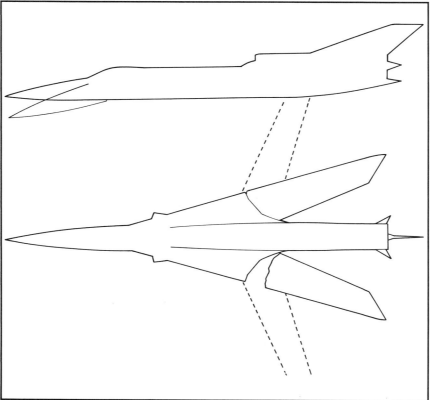

In retrospect it is unfortunate that the studies revolved around long-range attack missions, overseas deployment and, instead of true STOL capability, merely a runway requirement less demanding than that of the F-105. TAC had already studied the Zell (zero-length launch) technique in which combat aircraft are blasted like missiles off a launcher using a giant rocket; this was unattractive on such counts as flexibility, safety, convenience and cost. VTOL was all the rage in Europe, where some of the basic techniques had been sewn up in patents by Rolls-Royce and Bristol Aero-Engines Ltd, and this provoked a large measure of prejudice against it in TAC. It was commonly felt, and not without justification at that time, that a VTOL was too limited in range and weapon load to be much use. This was before the era of efficient STOVLs like Harrier II with its ski-jump technique.

So, instead of concentrating on what would happen when the Soviets fired the hundreds of their nuclear missiles which are targeted on NATO airfields, the USAF planners considered only attack by conventional bomb-dropping aircraft. They came up with the answer that any substantial improvement – such as 50 per cent – on the F-105 runway requirement would be most welcome. It became fashionable to talk of "taking off between the craters".

Leaping into the mid-1980s we now have the situation in which protesters campaign against the so-called 'cruise' as likely to invite nuclear retaliation,

despite the fact that no enemy can know its whereabouts in advance, while the alternative long-range delivery system in the European NATO context is the F-111 whose whereabouts are in general known to within a few metres. It seems common sense to equip an air force only with combat aircraft capable of dispersal away from nuclear rocket attack, but the evidence of discussion on this point in the TAC thinking of 1960 is hard to discover.

In contrast, there is abundant evidence that any real attempt to move

Above: The third and sixth RDT&E aircraft formating with wings at maximum sweep. Even at this stage they were quite different from 63-9766 seen opposite – and from each other.

Top left: Wing loading of all One-Elevens is high by any standard. This is fine for low-level attack but it makes the aircraft a bit of a non-starter where air combat is called for.

Top right: Power loading is gross weight divided by total engine thrust. Again, the One-Eleven's great weight makes it a 'non-fighter'.

Left: The original spur to NASA's swept-wing work was the swing-wing (and droop nose) work of Vickers-Armstrongs at Weybridge in 1958–9.

towards V/STOLs was thought undesirable. Not only was it thought to result in rather useless aircraft, but the problems of logistics and what later became known as C^3 (Command, Control and Communications) were considered to negate the advantages. No less an expert than the USAF Director of Operational Requirements, Major-General Bruce K. Holloway, said: "In order to disperse one or two flights at appreciable distances from each other we would require major changes in the supporting base structure. A fleet of VTOL supply aircraft would be required. A vastly increased communica-

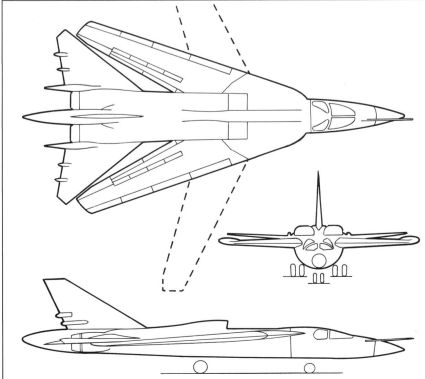

Left: The unpainted fourth prototype with anti-spin chute, full flap/slat deployment and four dummy Phoenix long-range air-to-air missiles.

Below left: Boeing-Wichita destroyed almost all their records on their excellent TFX submission. This three-view at least survives.

Above: The seventh RDT&E aircraft with wings at the minimum sweep angle of 16deg and carrying four dummy nuclear bombs.

Below: The first air-to-air picture at maximum sweep. It was secured on the same January 1965 sortie as the adjacent illustration.

Above: Another view of the seventh prototype on test with B61 'nukes'. The outer pylons, on the swinging wings, sometimes failed to pivot.

Below: For comparison with the picture opposite, this shows the dramatic way the F-111 can change its shape on command of the pilot.

tions net would also be necessary ...".

We cannot pursue the argument, because in almost a quarter century since that time little more has been done to make air power survivable on the ground. But 1959–60 was a crucial era in which the USAF had the power to steer the thinking of the world's air forces in this direction.

As it was, it was only after considerable argument that SOR-183 (Specific Operational Requirement) was drawn up in the first half of 1960. Nobody argued about the central demand, which was the ability to carry two nuclear weapons internally and fly at Mach 1·2 (912mph/1,468km/h) at treetop height over very long distances

to a major ground target. It was also agreed there had to be a considerable capability with conventional 'iron bombs', but here the bombload could vary from 5,000lb to 30,000lb (2,268kg to 13,608kg), and in 1960 the general view was that 10,000lb (4,536kg) was an acceptable minimum. Very curiously, as the aircraft was called a fighter, there appear to have been no numerical demands for SEP (specific excess power, a measure of surplus propulsive thrust available for the extra energy needed for climb or manoeuvring), or for turn radius or any other manoeuvre demands, and very limited and uncertain specification of air-to-air weapons.

Ultimately SOR-183 was issued on June 14, 1960, calling for a Future Tactical Strike Fighter. Somebody subsequently omitted the vital word 'strike' and it became Tactical Fighter Experimental or TFX. With hindsight it is self-evident that, as the entire emphasis of SOR-183 was on long-range attack, the aircraft ought really to have been called an attack aircraft, with a DoD number such as A-7 (pushing the 1964 Vought Corsair II down the list to become the A-8). This would have saved a fantastic amount of time, money and aggravation, because the new US Administration of John F. Kennedy which assumed office on January 20, 1961, brought with it a man determined to be a new broom to sweep the Pentagon clean: Robert S. McNamara.

A former Vice-President of the Ford Motor Co, McNamara was an incisive businessman who, probably rightly, believed the Pentagon to be a vast house peopled by costly bureaucrats who needed a good shakeup in order to deliver better value for money. Sadly, he also got involved in technical matters. He is quoted as watching a Navy flypast and asking "What good are all

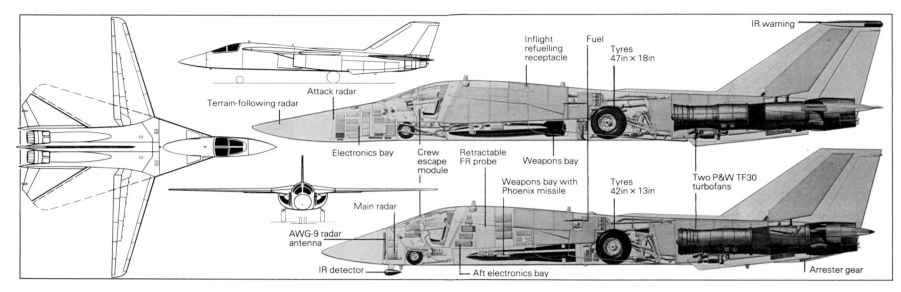

those different kinds of airplanes?" – the implied belief being that one, or possibly two, types could have flown all the Navy's missions. One of the first things he did on taking office was to be told all the biggest new DoD procurement programmes. He believed many could be combined, to the taxpayer's benefit.

It so happened that running in parallel with the USAF SOR-183 was a Navy programme called the Fleet Air Defense Fighter. This called for the longest possible time on CAP (Combat Air Patrol), armed with a heavy load of long-range AAMs and powerful radar to spot hostile aircraft at distances of at least 100 miles (160km). After many studies the Navy had discovered that, provided

Below: This beautiful 'profile' depicts the second production F-111B, the final example completed of the Navy version. We ought to shed no tears at its demise.

Above: Simple three-view of the F-111B. The main distinguishing feature was the non-Aardvark nose.

the AAM had sufficient flight performance, the carrier aircraft could almost be a modified S-2 with a speed of about 180mph (290km/h)! By 1959 the FADF had centred on the Douglas F6D Missileer, a subsonic aircraft with long mission endurance, the powerful Hughes AWG-9 radar and six or even eight of the giant Bendix Eagle AAMs. But many people could not understand the concept of a subsonic fighter, and in one of his last acts the outgoing Navy Secretary, Thomas S. Gates Jr, cancelled the F6D.

Above: Comparative inboard profiles of the F-111A (upper) and F-111B, published by GD on June 15, 1965.

Consequently, when McNamara was briefed on the TFX he was also briefed on the FADF, which was in a very fluid state. Many companies in the US industry were preparing proposals for either or both, and it seemed obvious that both TFX and FADF were going to be programmes of the first magnitude, together replacing such important types as the F-105, F-101, F-104, F-100, F-6, F-8, F-3, the new F-4 Phantom in all versions for all services, and also all derived reconnaissance models of each type. When Allied purchases were

added, the total production was likely to run into several thousand, and as a former Ford man McNamara believed in getting the price down by building lots of identical items.

Thus was born the drive for commonality between the TFX and FADF. Like many aspects of the F-111 story it has been aired in countless Congressional reports, hardback books and articles in the media throughout the world. Most readers will already know that, against almost all the professional advice of people in the Air Force and Navy, the new SecDef actually did bulldoze through a common programme for a new fighter for both services. He insisted on the maximum commonality

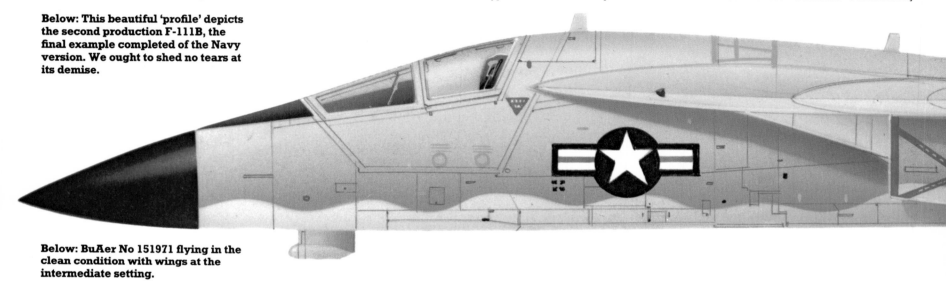

Below: BuAer No 151971 flying in the clean condition with wings at the intermediate setting.

even to the extent of personally telling the rival bidders how to design the aircraft.

The eventual winner, the Fort Worth Division of General Dynamics (GD), was selected – again in the face of almost all the expert opinion in the Air Force – largely because, even though its price was higher, it offered to build with a higher degree of commonality than the second-placed bidder. The latter was Boeing-Wichita, whose excellent engineering team lost out largely because it recognized that to meet what actually were two entirely different sets of requirements you have to build two different aircraft.

At all times the basic design was

of the very few 'fighters' ever built with side-by-side seats – certainly never saved the US taxpayer the anticipated billion dollars.

Also omitted from this book are details of the scandals which rocked not only Washington but the entire United States after the F-111 contract was awarded to GD on November 24, 1962. These began with the widespread belief that Mr McNamara had picked the wrong aircraft; as an official Report to the US Senate later stated, "The preliminary enquiry soon revealed that there was substantial reason to believe that the decision had been made to buy the second-best airplane at the higher price". This particular row raged for

Above: The first colour air-to-air of the first F-111B. Interesting that Grumman went for tandem seats in the F-14 Tomcat!

dictated primarily by the USAF requirement, the unfortunate Navy being instructed to demand the fewest possible essential changes. Thus the aircraft finally built was not significantly compromised by the Navy FAD mission except in the single matter of the cockpit arrangement. The Air Force had originally specified tandem seating for a pilot and WSO (weapon-system officer), which offered lower drag and better all-round view for both men. The Navy favoured side-by-side seating because this made it slightly less impossible for the 'common' design to meet the severe limitation on overall length for compatibility with aircraft carriers. The increased drag did not matter to a stand-off interceptor carrying AAMs with a range in the order of 100 miles (161km), and for most naval missions the side-by-side arrangement was actually an advantage.

Thus the F-111A for the Air Force and F-111B for the Navy were built with side-by-side seating. After agonizing problems the F-111B ground to a halt in 1968 and was replaced by the F-14, and it does not appear again in this book. But the legacy it left of arguments and problems – quite apart from being one

years, and has still not entirely subsided, though it was eventually surpassed in popular appeal by Watergate.

What was much more serious was that the F-111 itself ran into an extraordinary succession of serious technical difficulties. Not one of these stemmed from any of the radically new features in the design, but they combined to have a major effect on the overall programme. One effect was still further to reduce the capability of the F-111 as an air-combat fighter, to the extent that – though for purely emotional reasons today's F-111 jocks insist they are *fighter* crews, and regard the word 'bomber' as a studied insult – the aircraft has never been used in any kind of fighter role whatsoever. Another effect was that, in the sharpest contrast to the sausage-machine production envisaged by McNamara, the total programme comprised a mere 562 aircraft split up into batches of nine types.

Today the Royal Australian Air Force has 20 F-111C aircraft and four modified F-111As, while the USAF has one wing each of the F-111A, F-111D, F-111E and F-111F, and two squadron-size wings of the FB-111A. To make life harder, shortages of both aircraft and crucial spares

have resulted in some squadrons having to operate a mix of different sub-types, greatly increasing the cost and complicating training and maintenance.

Almost the only part of the programme that has worked more or less as planned has been the newest version, the unarmed EF-111A electronic-warfare aircraft. Here 42 F-111As are being completely rebuilt by Grumman, as described in the penultimate chapter. Earlier versions were procured in reduced numbers either in order to switch to an improved model or because of the effect of inflation on the purchase price.

Triumph in adversity

Thus, instead of being the global smash-hit that Mr McNamara and many other people expected in 1961, the F-111 programme has suffered many disappointments, amplified by the close attentions of a generally hostile press. Yet if only it were possible to forget the difficulties – and the unfortunate word 'fighter' which caused half the problems – no objective observer can but conclude that the F-111 will go down in history as an aircraft of immense stature and capability which ushered in a new

age in military aviation. Though the popular media often cannot see beyond its swing wings, that design feature is purely incidental. Its true importance lies in the fact that it was the first aircraft to make blind first-pass attacks on point targets, and to penetrate hostile airspace in the TF (terrain following) mode.

The first accomplishment means it can fly as straight as an arrow to a known fixed point on the ground, day or night and in any weather, and drop a bomb within a circle of maybe 50 metres radius. Both the TAC and SAC versions have such a string of success behind them in pinpoint navigation and bombing competitions that this capability is not in doubt. As a bonus, which in some theatres is vital, the range of the F-111 even without air refuelling handsomely exceeds that of any other military jet except large subsonic aircraft (the Soviet Su-24 is probably comparable). One has only to study the Su-24 to see that the Sukhoi designers have paid the engineers who created the F-111 the greatest of all compliments. They have probably been able to set up a better programme, however, building many hundreds of the same model.

Design

The fact that today's One-Elevens can do their job is testimony to the basic rightness of the design: however, nobody today would build the aircraft in this way. Even eliminating any suggestion that the aircraft has any air-combat capability, it would be preferable to use tandem seating, and with gross weights of 100,000lb and over the propulsive thrust could well be increased by at least 50 per cent. Alternatively the basic demands for mission radius and ferry range should have been pitched much lower. But the sincerest form of flattery is imitation, and the Soviet counterpart, the Su-24, is almost a copy!

SOR-183, the USAF document which launched the TFX programme which led to the F-111, merely spelled out a list of requirements. It did not specify how many engines, or even how many wings, the successful proposal aircraft might have; but at the same time the document itself was drawn up in a curious manner which virtually dictated that the successful design would have a swing wing.

Back in the early 1950s the US National Advisory Committee for Aeronautics, largely in the ebullient person of John Stack, chief of supersonic tunnels at the Langley Laboratory, had cast an attentive eye over the concept of the pivoted swing wing, or VG (variable-geometry) aircraft. No elegant way of using the idea seemed possible until October 1957, when a proposal came out of the blue from Vickers-Armstrongs (Aircraft) in Britain.

NACA had just begun a further study of swing wings when the US Mutual Weapons Development Program office in Paris advised Langley that a disgruntled Barnes Wallis at Vickers was looking for someone to replace the UK Ministry of Supply which had just abandoned the swing wing (because it had been decreed that manned combat aircraft were no longer going to be needed). To cut a very long story short

the end result was not funds going to Weybridge but the very considerable Vickers research information going to Stack.

In October 1958 NACA was renamed NASA (National Aeronautics and Space Administration), and by this time not only had Stack completed tunnel testing of a basic swing-wing shape but the Langley model-makers were being given drawings of possible future fighter shapes. Stack spent much of his time in heated discussion with planemakers, and almost as much in the company of generals. By this time he was Langley's Deputy Director, and probably the most important man in the Western world when it came to getting new aerodynamics into practical de-

signs of aircraft. He played a central role from the very start in helping Gen Everest draft the SOR-183 requirements, and the numbers stipulated stemmed directly from Langley's results in tunnel testing swing-wing models.

The key features in the Vickers-derived NASA configuration were: the left and right wings were each pivoted far outboard from the aircraft centreline, the pivots being fixed (many earlier ideas featured sliding wing roots) even well beyond the sides of the broad fuselage; inboard of the pivoted swing-wings was to be a large, acutely swept fixed portion called a glove; and the wing was mounted high so that the two gloves and the upper surface of the broad fuselage formed a large lifting

surface, which with the pivoted wings folded fully back would provide more than half the total lift. The range of sweep angles adopted by GD, which was typical of all the NASA studies and rival bidders, was 16deg to 72·5deg.

It is one of the larger examples of the dictates of fashion in aircraft design that the swing wing was so universally regarded as a panacea in 1960, eagerly adopted by all the six bidders on the TFX programme, yet so widely discounted in the Western world today. Naturally, the F-111 was such a major advance in the design of military aircraft that it was virtually copied by the Soviet Union; moreover TsAGI, the Moscow-centred aerodynamics institute, also perfected a configuration for turning swept-wing aircraft into swing-wing ones and this has been used in the Sukhoi single-engined attack family (derived from the Su-7) and the Tupolev supersonic bomber family (derived initially from the Tu-22). For the past several years there have been conferences at TsAGI and even at the Kremlin to reaffirm that the swing wing is frequently the best answer despite its non-

Above: The reason for the swing-wing is that, ideally, a transonic low-level attacker can almost lift itself on the fuselage!

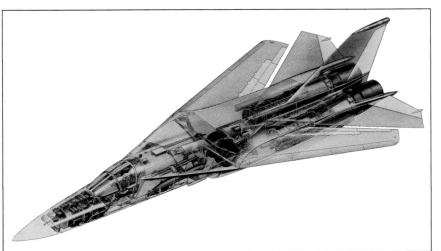

Below: British Aerospace tear 'em apart and rebuild 'em: UH = Es from Upper Heyford's 20th TFW, and LN = Fs from Lakenheath's 48th TFW.

Left: Long before first flight GD put out this cutaway F-111A showing a Bullpup ASM and two Sidewinder AAMs in the internal weapon bay!

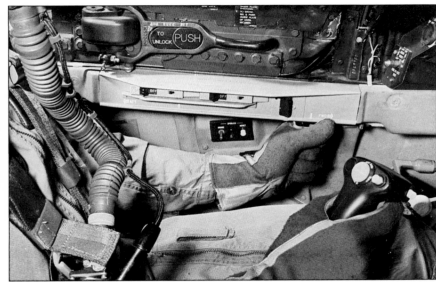

Top: A triple exposure in one of the Fort Worth refrigerated 'torture chambers' showing the way the wings were bent in proof testing.

Above: Close-up of the swing-wing pivot junction, showing how the glove vane rotates nose-down while its bottom half opens like a book.

Top: A GD engineering pilot grasps the 'trombone handle' which commands wing sweep angle. There is nothing to show which way is right!

Above: An F-111D of the 27th TFW shows the complex geometry of the slat, glove vane and pivot junction in the minimum-sweep position.

appearance in all the latest Western military aircraft except the B-1B, whose roots go back to the late 1960s when the swing wing was fashionable.

Variable geometry

It may not always be apparent that an aircraft of fixed shape has to be designed to perform at its best at one particular combination of flight speed, atmospheric density/temperature, aircraft weight and engine power setting. If any of these things (and a few others) is altered, the aircraft becomes less efficient. Half a century ago the first major elements of variable geometry were adopted in the form of leading-edge slats (which open to keep the air flowing back across the upper surface of the wing at high angles, for example at low speeds) and trailing-edge flaps (which when lowered slightly give a considerable increase in wing lift, and when lowered fully also cause a large increase in drag). Such forms of variable geometry are universally accepted; indeed in modern fighters the ability continuously to vary the wing cross-section profile to suit different speeds, manoeuvres or other flight conditions is put forward by their designers as a good alternative to the swing wing.

In fact, while variable wing profile is a powerful method of adapting the aircraft to changing conditions, it cannot possibly be regarded as a replacement for the swing wing. The latter offers an even more powerful means of, in effect, redesigning the aircraft in flight to fit it to different parts of a mission. At takeoff the wings are spread out at the maximum span, and the high-lift devices comprising full-span leading-edge slats and full-span trailing-edge double-slot-

ted flaps are all extended; in addition, the outer portion of fixed glove is opened into upper and lower portions, the lower forming a near-vertical guide vane around the inboard end of the slats and the upper (called the glove vane) being rotated nose-down to guide airflow over the wing above the inboard end of the slats, rather in the way a Kruger flap guides airflow at the wing root of a modern jetliner.

Cleaned up after takeoff the ugly duckling turns into a graceful swan, long-necked and with long slender wings considerably more efficient in subsonic cruise than the stubby wings of fixed-wing fighters – and, in fact, even more efficient than the wings of many jetliners! A typical cruise setting is 26deg, or 10deg of added sweep. This lines up the fixed outermost pylons with the airflow and is the only setting at which it is possible to carry the maximum external load. To sweep the wings further it is necessary to jettison the outermost pylons, if these are fitted (they seldom are). It would be possible to incorporate a Mach/sweep programmer to adjust wing sweep automatically to flight Mach number or some other parameter, but as in practice the F-111 is not intended to indulge in air combat there is no incentive to do so. Maximum sweep is needed only for supersonic dash, and though Mach numbers exceeding 2 are attainable at over 35,000ft (10,700m) the more familiar regime is at low level, invariably below 1,000ft (300m) AGL (above ground level) and in heavily defended areas below 300ft (90m), where hostile radars may be expected to have blinkered and unreliable vision.

Penetration of hostile territory was

recognised as early as 1944 to call for flight at the lowest possible altitude, to escape detection by radar until the last possible moment and give the defenders minimum warning and many other problems, but it was not until the 1950s that a few design teams were given the chance to come up with designs for dedicated low-level bombers. Such aircraft are a class apart, and in many respects their design has to be the exact opposite of that of an air-combat fighter. Thus, it is sheer nonsense to claim that machines such as the F-15, F/A-18A or Mirage 2000 can be 'designed' to fly both the fighter and the attack missions.

Immutable laws

Publicity managers can get very hot under the collar, but unfortunately they do not have the power with their press releases to alter the fact that the fighter needs the biggest wing it can get, while the attack aircraft needs the smallest. Not only does the attack aircraft need the highest possible wing loading (aircraft weight divided by wing area, in other words the average weight supported by each bit of wing) but it also needs the smallest possible span. Ideally it would like a mere sliver of a wing, with maximum chord (front to rear distance) but hardly any span. Imagine an F/A-18A with just its long wing-root extension, and with the main wing removed: that is the kind of shape that does well in penetrating hostile airspace at supersonic speed at treetop height.

The F/A-18 driver does not have the ability to remove his main wings, except with dire consequences, but this is just what the swing-wing jock can do by the

mere touch of a lever. Sweeping the F-111 outer wings back to 72·5deg has only a modest effect on the total area but a dramatic effect on the span, which is reduced to around half its maximum value. Why is it important to change the shape of the wing in this way? There are five main reasons, but the chief one is that not only is drag greatly reduced, so the aircraft can fly faster than sound, but also the variation of lift with AOA (angle of attack) is greatly reduced.

AOA is the angle at which the wing meets the air. A normal unswept wing held at near-zero AOA will give no lift at all. As AOA is increased, while holding airspeed constant, so does the lift increase in a fairly uniform way until, at an AOA of around 16deg, the wing runs out of steam. It then cannot lift any more (not without increase in airspeed, which at high AOA means tremendous increase in engine thrust), and any attempt to increase AOA further will result in a stall, the aircraft dropping like a stone. The slender wing, such as an F-111 at 72·5deg, shows very much less variation in lift with AOA; it is said to have a 'flat lift-curve' when the results are plotted on a graph. It so happens that AOA can be increased to seemingly crazy angles without the aircraft dropping out of the sky, but these are not part of an F-111 driver's normal repertoire.

The crucial advantage of a flat lift-curve is that, since the air at low levels is both very dense and very turbulent, because of the effect of wind on hills, buildings and other terrain features, a high-speed attacker inevitably finds his wings flying through an endless succession of upcurrents and downcurrents of an unpredictable nature. This means that AOA is constantly changing in a

Above: Crew modules from McDonnell Douglas lined up at Fort Worth for installation. Each cost as much as a complete F-86.

Below: Three landing and taxi lights adorn the nose gear, which has twin steerable wheels. It folds forward, pulling the doors after it.

Bottom: This crew module was seen on inspection in the Fort Worth plant prior to being built into 63-9783, the eighteenth Research, Development,

Test and Evaluation aircraft, which was subsequently rebuilt as the first prototype FB-111A for Strategic Air Command.

random and often violent manner. With a normal (long-span) wing the ride is so rough that, to use aircrew parlance, "you get your eyeballs shaken out". In contrast the F-111 or Tornado or Soviet aircrew have a smooth ride, and can fly their mission with professional precision. (The only other kind of aircraft that can do this is the TSR.2 type with extremely high wing-loading in a short-span wing, rather like a swing wing at maximum sweep, and with very powerful flap blowing to get enough lift for takeoff and landing.)

We in the West must be careful not to forget that such recent aircraft as the F-16, F/A-18 and Mirage 2000 have fixed wings not as a matter of fundamental choice. These aircraft were originally designed for the air-combat mission; and, having been thus designed, their wings could not readily be given pivots. Their manufacturers thus have a vested interest in trying to avoid discussion of their limitations in the attack mission.

To be frank, if a fixed-wing aircraft slows down to about 450 knots and maintains a good height AGL – say, 1,000ft (300m) – it can fly a respectable attack mission, such as that achieved by

F-16s against a nuclear reactor in Iraq. In missions over the sea, which is flat and has relatively unturbulent air above it, the F/A-18A can fly a fair attack mission at the same speed at considerably lower heights. But put any fixed-wing aircraft on the Central European NATO front, and it becomes a totally different ball game. Indeed, put it on a mission against Hanoi in the early 1970s and it would find low-level flight on a cloudy night through the mountains with rings of SAM batteries ahead to be an unacceptable situation. No amount of hard-sell shouting can alter the laws of nature. Certainly, we must guard against thinking the swing wing outmoded.

At the same time, though the F-111 will forever be remembered as the first production swing-wing aircraft, it is certainly not above criticism. GD cannot be blamed for the side-by-side seating, which in 1962 became inevitable, but in many other respects the design left much to be desired. US interest in the BAC (which absorbed Vickers-Armstrongs) swing-wing and TSR.2 research, all of which was passed to the USAF, triggered corresponding BAC interest in TFX, and when B.O. Heath at

Far left: The left taileron (stabilator) of an F-111F, parked at full positive incidence. Note the ECM aerial and static dischargers located on the trailing edge.

Left: The high-lift devices of an F-111F are clarified by the distinctive red paint of the internals. The flaps in this photograph are not at maximum deflection.

Below left: White number 5 is for RAF Strike Command's Tactical Bomb Competition, held at Lossiemouth: this 48th TFW F-111F was taking part in 1981.

BAC Warton saw a three-view of the F-111 he thought it worth writing a brief critique. He pointed out that it was undesirable to have the tailplane at the same level as the wing, so that the wing and tailplane almost became one surface at 72·5deg sweep; that the wing pivots were not in "quite the right place"; that there was too much length of body upstream of the inlets, so that a thick boundary-layer of sluggish air would have to be disposed of inboard of the inlets; that the inlets were too close to the engines, so that distorted airflow would be likely to cause serious engine compressor stalls; and that base drag at the tail would be excessive.

It so happened that the British government later threw away Heath's own aircraft (TSR.2) and regarded the F-111 as the perfect replacement, completely ignoring this critical appraisal. But everything Heath predicted was proved to be true, and in addition he might have added that it is undesirable and unnecessary to design main landing gears which make it impossible to carry a heavy weapon, tank or ECM load under the fuselage. Heath later played a central role in the design of the much smaller Tornado which regularly carries an 8,000lb (3629kg) bombload without having to use a single wing pylon.

Ejectable capsule

One of the most unusual features of the F-111 is that instead of having ejection seats the crew ride in an ejectable capsule. The only company with previous experience of ejectable capsules on a production aircraft was GD Fort Worth itself, with the B-58, which had three in a row. The F-111 has just the one capsule, inside which is the complete side-by-side cockpit. McDonnell Douglas played the prime role in developing this so-called 'crew module'. In emergency either occupant can grab a lever beside his knee and, with a press-squeeze-pull movement, initiate the jettison sequence. Explosive cutting cord severs the module from the aircraft, and a 40,000lb (18,000kg) thrust rocket zooms it up and back at any flight Mach number down to zero and at any height.

A large portion of wing goes with the module to give inflight stability, the internal pressurization is discontinued but oxygen supply is maintained, and the controlled descent is retarded by a parachute with impact cushioned by ventral airbags. There are cases of crews surviving with nothing more than a shaking after a capsule has rolled down a craggy mountainside. On land the capsule forms a survival shelter; on sea it behaves like a self-righting boat, the pilot's stick serving as the handle of the bilge-pump!

The troubled development history of the F-111 is well known, and it is unpre-cedented for a single modern combat aircraft to have suffered so severely on the counts of excessive aerodynamic drag, engine/inlet mismatch (to the point that the TF30 engine installation was officially described as "a hazard to safe flight"), excessive weight, shortfalls in range, speed and height, and, later, catastrophic structural failures. Coming on top of the thundering row over the contract award, with its overtones of incompetence and individual self-interest among the highest members of the Defense Department, all this had a most damaging effect on what was actually a very fine aircraft.

Above: Flightline of the 48th TFW at the 1981 Tac Bombing Contest. The F-111 (even the F) has to try hard today to beat the F-16!

In retrospect the author still believes that the SOR-183 figures were ill-conceived from the start. The ferry range without air refuelling was stipulated at 3,000nm (3,455 miles/5,560km); this was responsible for GD having to show in-

Below: Basic features of the unique jettisonable crew module. The bilge pump is driven by the joysticks should the module land in water.

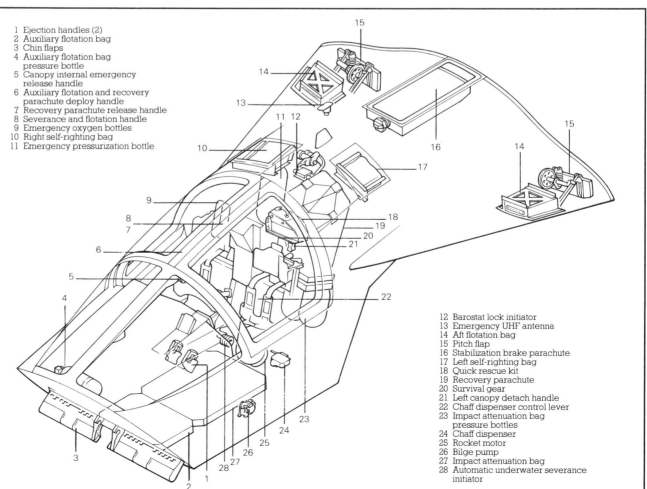

1 Ejection handles (2)
2 Auxiliary flotation bag
3 Chin flaps
4 Auxiliary flotation bag pressure bottle
5 Canopy internal emergency release handle
6 Auxiliary flotation and recovery parachute deploy handle
7 Recovery parachute release handle
8 Severance and flotation handle
9 Emergency oxygen bottles
10 Right self-righting bag
11 Emergency pressurization bottle
12 Barostat lock initiator
13 Emergency UHF antenna
14 Aft flotation bag
15 Pitch flap
16 Stabilization brake parachute
17 Left self-righting bag
18 Quick rescue kit
19 Recovery parachute
20 Survival gear
21 Left canopy detach handle
22 Chaff dispenser control lever
23 Impact attenuation bag pressure bottles
24 Chaff dispenser
25 Rocket motor
26 Bilge pump
27 Impact attenuation bag
28 Automatic underwater severance initiator

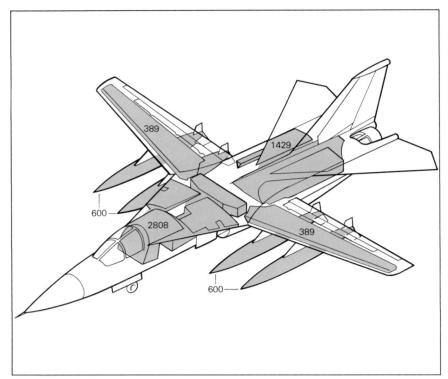

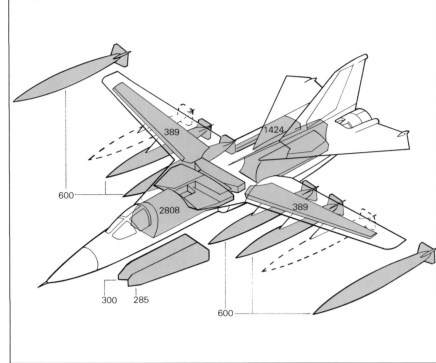

Above: Based on a USAF illustration, this diagram shows the fuel tanks of an F-111A or E (most tactical versions are similar). The figures are capacities in US gallons: the main cutaway drawing below gives corresponding capacities in Imperial gallons and litres.

Above: An equivalent diagram showing the tankage of the FB-111A bomber, with optional weapon-bay tanks (and 5US gal less internal).

F-111D cutaway

1 Hinged nose cone
2 Attack radar
3 Terrain-following radar
4 Nose hinges (2)
5 Radar mounting
6 Nose lock
7 Angle-of-sideslip probe
8 Homing antenna (high)
9 Forward warning antenna
10 Homing antenna (low and mid)
11 ALR-41 antenna
12 Flight control computers
13 Feel and trim assembly
14 Forward avionics bay (Advanced Mk II digital computer)
15 Angle-of-attack probe
16 UHF Comm/Tacan No 2
17 Module forward bulkhead and stabilization flaps (2)
18 Twin nosewheels
19 Shock strut
20 Underfloor impact attenuation bag stowage (4)
21 Nosewheel well
22 LOX converter
23 Rudder pedals
24 Control column
25 LOX heat exchanger
26 Auxiliary flotation bag pressure bottle
27 Weapons sight
28 Forward parachute bridle line
29 De-fog nozzle
30 Windscreen
31 Starboard console
32 Emergency oxygen bottle
33 Crew seats
34 Bulkhead console
35 Wing sweep control handle
36 Recovery chute catapult
37 Provision/survival pack
38 Attenuation bags pressure bottle
39 Recovery chute
40 Aft parachute bridle line
41 UHF data link/AGIFF No 1 (see 123)
42 Stabilization-brake chute
43 Self-righting bag
44 UHF recovery
45 ECM antennae (port and starboard)
46 Forward fuselage fuel bay (2,340lmp gal/10,638litres)
47 Ground refuelling receptacle
48 Weapons bay
49 Module pitch flaps (port and starboard.
50 Aft flotation bag stowage
51 Air refuelling receptacle
52 Primary heat-exchanger (air-to-water)
53 Ram air inlet
54 Rate gyros
55 Rotating glove
56 Inlet variable spike

57 Port intake
58 Air brake/undercarriage door
59 Auxiliary inlet blow-in doors
60 Rotating glove pivot point
61 Inlet vortex generators
62 Wing sweep pivot
63 Wing centre-box assembly
64 Wing sweep actuator
65 Wing sweep feedback
66 Control runs
67 Rotating glove drive set
68 Inboard pivot pylons (2)
69 Auxiliary drop tanks (500lmp gal/2,273litres)
70 Outboard fixed pylon (subsonic/jettisonable)
71 Slat drive set
72 Wing fuel tank (324lmp gal/1,473 litres)
73 Leading-edge slat
74 Starboard navigation light
75 Flap drive set
76 Outboard spoiler actuator
77 Starboard spoilers
78 Inboard spoiler actuator
79 Flaps
80 Wing swept position
81 Auxiliary flap
82 Auxiliary flap actuator
83 Nuclear weapons and weapons control equipment package
84 Wing sweep/Hi Lift control box
85 Flap, slat and glove drive mechanism
86 Starboard engine bay
87 Yaw feel spring
88 Roll feel spring
89 Yaw trim actuator
90 Yaw damper servo
91 Roll stick position transducer
92 Pitch trim actuator (manual)
93 Roll damper servo
94 Pitch trim actuator (series)
95 Pitch feel spring
96 Pitch-roll mixer
97 Pitch damper servo
98 Pitch stick position transducer
99 Aft fuselage frames
100 Aft fuselage fuel bays (1,191lmp gal/5,413litres)
101 Horizontal stabilizer servo actuator
102 Starboard horizontal stabilizer
103 Aft warning antennae
104 HF antenna
105 Detector scanner
106 X-Band radar
107 Rudder
108 Integral vent tank
109 Fin aft spar
110 Fin structure

Above: An F-111D of the 27th TFW undergoing hangar maintenance at Cannon AFB, near Clovis, New Mexico, in August 1981.

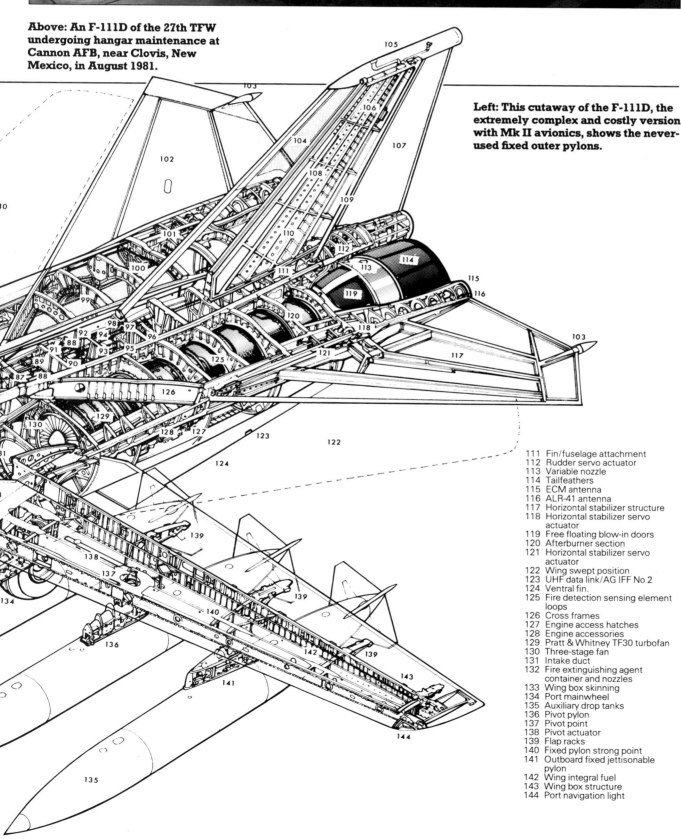

Left: This cutaway of the F-111D, the extremely complex and costly version with Mk II avionics, shows the never-used fixed outer pylons.

111 Fin/fuselage attachment
112 Rudder servo actuator
113 Variable nozzle
114 Tailfeathers
115 ECM antenna
116 ALR-41 antenna
117 Horizontal stabilizer structure
118 Horizontal stabilizer servo actuator
119 Free floating blow-in doors
120 Afterburner section
121 Horizontal stabilizer servo actuator
122 Wing swept position
123 UHF data link/AG IFF No 2
124 Ventral fin
125 Fire detection sensing element loops
126 Cross frames
127 Engine access hatches
128 Engine accessories
129 Pratt & Whitney TF30 turbofan
130 Three-stage fan
131 Intake duct
132 Fire extinguishing agent container and nozzles
133 Wing box skinning
134 Port mainwheel
135 Auxiliary drop tanks
136 Pivot pylon
137 Pivot point
138 Pivot actuator
139 Flap racks
140 Fixed pylon strong point
141 Outboard fixed jettisonable pylon
142 Wing integral fuel
143 Wing box structure
144 Port navigation light

genuity in packing fuel into every last nook and cranny apart from the fin, with a consequent rise in takeoff weight on the conventional (HE) mission to over 100,000lb (45.36 tonnes). The demand for Mach 2.5 at high altitude resulted in prolonged tinkering with inlets, and in fact was never met even with the much more powerful F-111F because it reduces airframe life and appears to have been quite unnecessary (it was written in largely because of the belief that the F-111 would be used for high-altitude fighter and reconnaissance missions). Not least, the TAC baseline mission of an attack on a surface target at a distance of 800nm (921 miles/1,482km) stipulated that the final 200nm to the target should be flown at Mach 1.2; though the fuel for the required ferry mission could marginally also meet this demand it caused numerous problems and, of course, was impossible with a conventional bombload.

It is easy to be wise after the event, but it is difficult to avoid the conclusion that it has always been folly to write a specification for a strategic bomber (according to McNamara "with the range of a transport") and expect it also to be a superior aircraft in any kind of fighter mission. The extremely severe problems encountered in development, including massive deficiency in aircraft range, ceiling, speed and manoeuvrability, could not have been predicted – because, despite a background research programme exceeding that for any previous aircraft of its size in history, none of these things *was* discovered in advance. There appears to be some justification for the oft-repeated American belief that it is better to design a world-beating fighter and then hang bombs on it, though the European experience with Tornado and Viggen shows that the reverse is possible if the basic design is a success.

Another of the bits of mythology that has grown up around the One-Eleven is that, while the Navy was crippled by weight restrictions, the Air Force was unconcerned. In a standard hardback reference, *McNamara: His Ordeal in the Pentagon* (Harper & Row, 1971) the author, Henry L. Trewhitt, writes "the Air Force wanted a plane that weighed no less than 75,000 pounds (34,000kg) ..." In fact during the crucial years of SOR-183 the thinking in TAC was that a way had to be found to keep the weight down to levels with which the command was familiar. The actual target gross weight in June 1959 was 45,000lb (20,412kg), and Gen Everest is on record as saying "I am not going to accept any goddamned 70,000-lb (31,750kg) airplane". As late as December 1961, well into the unprecedented four rounds of competitive bidding by the rival contractors, Everest with extreme reluctance agreed to raise the absolute upper limit on gross weight to 60,000lb (27,216kg), and only as a last-ditch tradeoff in order to achieve the desired lo-lo-hi penetration radius of 800nm.

There is no doubt whatsoever that it is the difference between weights of this order and those actually reached by the production versions of F-111 that effectively killed the aircraft as a fighter. Indeed, one feels there must have been some optimism on the part of the contractors or a gross breakdown in communications for the customer to fix an absolute upper limit at 60,000lb for an aircraft that fully laden turns the scales at various levels (depending on subtype) between 98,850 and 119,243lb (44,838 and 54,088kg). But, conversely, it is these awesome weights that give the F-111 its still-unrivalled range/bombload combination for a tactical aircraft.

Powerplant

One of the key technological advances which made possible the concept of the TFX was the high-compression augmented turbofan, which can combine very high maximum thrust with fuel economy far better than for the older generation of turbojets. Pratt & Whitney won the potentially enormous job of powering the F-111 with the promising TF30. The dour and conservative engine supplier suffered beyond belief in this programme (and in others using this engine), not least because of the design of the aircraft inlet system. The result was a succession of new TF30 models, combined with crippling price inflation.

Among the many curious facets of the F-111 design is that although the USAF never stipulated two engines, no contractor ever submitted any other number. The aircraft TFX was intended to replace, above all others, was the single-engined F-105. The engine of the F-105 was a large and extremely robust two-spool turbojet augmented by a large afterburner with a fully variable multi-flap nozzle. In its day it was a fine engine, and in fact the same engine minus the afterburner has today been refurbished and used in the TR-1. But by the end of the 1950s the advent of the turbofan, pioneered by Rolls-Royce under the name 'bypass turbojet', opened the way to superior fuel economy.

To a first approximation the fuel consumption of a jet engine of given power depends upon the mean jet velocity. At subsonic speeds it pays to use an engine that handles a larger airflow and discharges it at lower velocity, though compared with a high-velocity simple turbojet such an engine is likely to be larger, heavier and more complicated. In fighters it is often not just fuel consumption that matters but the total weight of the powerplant plus the fuel burned in each mission that determines how the aircraft is designed. For a lightweight air-combat fighter the need for agility in combat may well outweigh the need for range, and it pays to use a simple engine even though it burns more fuel. In the case of the F-111 quite the opposite considerations applied.

Never before had such range been demanded of any fighter-type aircraft. It was clear from the outset that the propulsion equations more nearly resembled those of a supersonic bomber, where the increased size and complexity of a high-compression turbofan handling a large airflow are amply rewarded in reduced weight of fuel consumed.

Turbofan advantages

Compared with a turbojet, a turbofan extracts more power from the jet with additional stages of turbine blading and uses this power either to drive a separate fan at the rear or a greatly enlarged low-pressure compressor at the front. In either case, the added fan blades pump fresh air which does not pass through the rest of the engine but is discharged as a relatively slow-moving cooler jet surrounding the hot 'core jet' from the rest of the engine.

Not only does this reduce the mean velocity of the combined hot central jet and surrounding fan jet, thus reducing fuel consumption, but it has the bonus of dramatically reduced noise. Moreover, as the air in the surrounding fan jet still has all its oxygen (because no fuel has been burned in it) it is possible to burn a great deal of extra fuel in it to give very large thrust boost for supersonic flight. In ordinary turbojets the afterburner is fed not with fresh air but with already very hot gas whose oxygen has partly been consumed. Thus an ordinary afterburner cannot burn much additional fuel before either the oxygen is all used up or the temperature becomes excessive. One of the chief technical advances in the engines of the F-111 was that, for the first time, an efficient turbofan was combined with a thrust-boosting augmentation system which injected fuel into both the hot core jet (as in previous afterburners) and also into the fresh air compressed by the fan.

Turbofans had been built previously, but only for subsonic bombers and transports. For the F-111 the engine had to be cleared to Mach 2·5 in the stratosphere and – an even more severe demand – to operate at sea level for

Above: The whole engine slides out to the rear, the variable nozzle always being outside the aircraft. Here an 18,500lb thrust TF30-P-3 is checked over for an F-111E of the 20th TFW at RAF Upper Heyford.

long periods at a sustained supersonic Mach number of 1·2. It went without saying that the overall propulsion system would have fully variable inlets, as well as the variable nozzle forming part of the engine itself.

One reason for the choice of two engines was to provide a degree of twin-engine safety. Modern engines are reliable, but the F-111 was clearly going to spend much of its life at low level where birdstrikes are a major hazard, causing expensive shedding of blades and either loss of an engine or at least a precautionary shutdown. Another reason was that total thrust for takeoff or Mach 1·2 dash was going to be approximately 40,000lb (18,000kg), and nobody

Below: What Americans call afterburner (usually abbreviated to 'burner) is often called reheat in Britain, though the strict term for a turbofan is augmentation. RAAF F-111C.

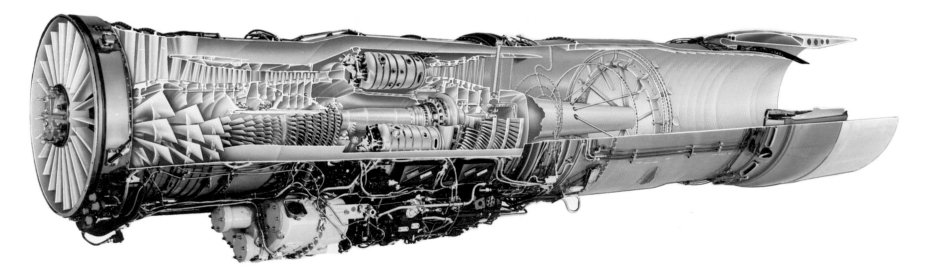

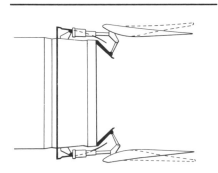

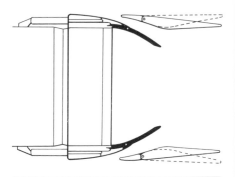

had built a production military engine of this size. In contrast, 20,000lb (9,000kg) was a handy and familiar size, well suited to field engine-change operations without outsize handling gear.

It was logical for bidders to place the engines side-by-side, with sufficient space between them for considerable fuselage fuel (though the largest tanks tended to be further forward, aft of the cockpit). How the inlets should be arranged was up to the aircraft designer. One of the best inlets on a USAF supersonic fighter had been the striking dorsal installation of the F-107A, and most bidders, including GD, studied inlets in the top of the fuselage.

The losing finalist, Boeing-Wichita, proposed to use dorsal inlets, and these would have had many advantages including reduced sensitivity to FOD (foreign-object damage) and possibly to birdstrikes. Another would certainly have been reduced RCS (radar cross-section), because engine inlets are among the most reflective parts of any aircraft and those on the F-111 today enable the hostile radars to 'see' right inside to the fronts of the engines. Another of the unexplained puzzles of the F-111 is that, in his explanation to Congress of why he picked the GD design, SecDef McNamara specifically mentioned the low RCS of that bidder's proposal, yet it must surely have been higher than for the Boeing aircraft with 'invisible' inlets?

In practice there were three candidate engines: the Allison AR.168, General Electric MF-295 and Pratt & Whitney JTF10. The Allison was based squarely on the Rolls-Royce Spey. Had it been chosen it would probably have

Top: A beautiful Pratt & Whitney artwork showing the fundamentally improved TF30-P-100, which powers the final new-build One-Eleven, the F. Hardly any part is unchanged from the earlier models.

Above left: One of the areas of total redesign in the P-100 is the variable nozzle (bottom), with a translating primary iris replacing the original flaps (top) and giving a consequent reduction in drag.

Above: A production TF30-P-3 is checked before delivery in 1967.

Right: Tank boom operator's view of an FB-111A during inflight refuelling.

filled the bill beautifully, with no significant trouble, but its 'foreign' origin prevented it from being judged on its merits. The MF-295 was possibly the most advanced of the three engines, but it existed only on paper and was finally deemed 'unacceptable' by the SSSB (Systems Source Selection Board). Boeing had preferred the GE engine but was given a paid study contract to switch to P&W, whose engine had originally been designed for the stillborn DC-9 four-engined passenger liner of 1958. For the F-111 the proposal was designated JTF10A-20, with a completely new afterburner and multi-flap nozzle. Accessories were grouped underneath, one of them being a large 60-kVA alternator (on both engines). Cartridge starting is possible, but the usual method is pneumatic, by air turbine, with cross-bleed to start the second engine.

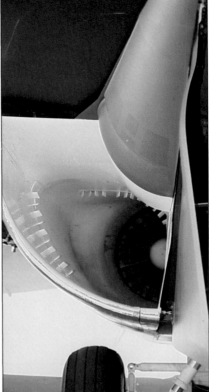

Above: Takeoff, in this case by an FB-111A, momentarily has the engines at full power fighting the vast barn-door airbrake which encloses the gear.

The Connecticut company's slogan had always been "Dependable engines", and in the F-111 engine it stuck to its principles of accepting greater engine weight than its rivals in order to secure solid reliability. This belief that the JTF10 would give less trouble than the alternative candidate engines was the chief factor in its choice. Designated TF30-P-1 it was on test by mid-1964, and two flight-cleared engines were installed in the first YF-111A at the ceremonial rollout on October 16, 1964, 16 days ahead of schedule. All went well on the first flight, but on Flight No 2, on January 6, 1965, Dick Johnson attempted to exceed Mach 1 with the wings fully swept and found severe compressor stall as soon as he tried accelerating in full afterburner.

Engine aerodynamics
The hundreds of blades in the fans and compressors of modern jet engines are each like a small wing, and subject to the same rules, though with the added complication that the flow past any one blade is determined by the blades upstream and downstream. Suppose the air downstream cannot get through the narrow, constricted high-pressure blades fast enough: this will slow up the flow in the early stages, and the angle of attack of each blade can become excessive, causing it to stall. Any sudden turbulence can trigger a stall, and a stall in one part of a compressor can quickly cause general breakdown of flow.

Compressor stalls can be violent; they can sound like major explosions to the pilot, and in extreme cases they result in the engine spewing broken blades out of the jetpipe. Designers therefore leave a clear 'stall margin' so that, in normal operation, a compressor stall just cannot happen. But the bigger the stall margin, the higher the fuel consumption. In trying to make their engine more efficient the P&W en-

Right: Tail-on aspect of a torn-down aircraft (being rebuilt into an EF). Ahead of the main inlet frame the inlet ducts curve outwards, with the inner walls covered in vortex vanes to re-energize boundary-layer airflow.

gineers had cut it too fine, and hewed too close to the stall line for the short F-111 inlet system.

P&W jet engines have almost as much flight time as those of all other Western makers combined, but experience and conservative design do not always result in a troublefree product. It is fair to assess the basically excellent TF30 as the most troublesome engine of the past 20 years, and the Navy is still seeking a replacement in the F-14. In the F-111 it retained its position as the sole engine, but only by being developed through eight main models (including one for the Navy F-111B) and with price-escalation of more than 300 per cent.

The first main variant to overcome the more critical shortcomings of the P-1 was the P-3 (Air Force engines have odd-numbered suffixes). This has a re-designed stator inlet, compressor spools spinning at different speeds from

the P-1 and with changed blade angles, a sixth-stage bleed to improve stall tolerance in combat manoeuvres or at supersonic speeds, a new afterburner fuel system, and modified nozzle. Still the engines coughed, banged and spluttered, and several losses of aircraft were attributed to engine behaviour.

GD discovered that much of the trouble lay in their inlet system, which – as predicted by 'Ollie' Heath in far-away Lancashire – was failing to get rid of the large boundary-layer flow and deliver smooth non-turbulent air to the very touchy engine. Engineers at Fort Worth spent four years improving the F-111 inlet system, despite the fact that an unprecedented effort had been applied to get it right at the outset.

The first major redesign was called Triple Plow I. Most unusually, the inlet that had been adopted for the F-111 took the form of a quarter-circle, with

Above: The original Triple Plow 1 inlet (F-111A, E and EF) has a large splitter plate close to the fuselage.

quarter of a conical centrebody, the location being well back under the wing root. The whole inlet was positioned outboard of the fuselage, from which it was separated by a large vertical wall. In Triple Plow I it was again moved a small further distance outboard, standing away from this wall, with a third plow (plough) to extract boundary layer between the top panel and the underside of the wing.

This remained the inlet for the F-111A, which was the most numerous variant, but by late 1967 GD had perfected a better Triple Plow II inlet with 14sq in (90sq cm) more area, positioned 4in (10cm) further out from the fuselage, with a longer and reprofiled corner cone to improve behaviour at high AOA

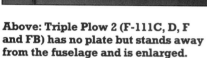

Above: Triple Plow 2 (F-111C, D, F and FB) has no plate but stands away from the fuselage and is enlarged.

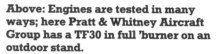

Above: Engines are tested in many ways; here Pratt & Whitney Aircraft Group has a TF30 in full 'burner on an outdoor stand.

and enabling the full Mach 2·5 performance to be realized at high altitude. This inlet also introduced three suck-in auxiliary doors in the wall about 12in (30cm) downstream, and it went into production for the F-111E. Unfortunately, as this retained the original engine it has insufficient power to reach this Mach number, and the vehemently expressed belief of the Senate TFX Investigation that there should have been "a constructive decision to stop F-111 production" pending the arrival of the Triple Plow II inlet appears unwarranted.

This inlet did, however, make possible the introduction of new versions of the TF30 which gradually made up some of the gross deficiency in power/weight ratio resulting from the massive escalation in F-111 weight. Discounting the stillborn Navy version, the next major advance in propulsion came in 1969 with the P-7 engine for the SAC bomber version, the FB-111A. This incorporates small changes, and has turbine entry temperature limit raised from 2,050deg F (1,121deg C) to 2,100deg F (1,149deg C) and rotational speeds appreciably increased (*see main data section, p000*). In the same year the P-9 succeeded the P-3 as powerplant of the basic TAC models, but this was fitted only to the F-111D. Turbine temperature is the same as for the P-7, but further increase in rotational speed results in increased thrust.

All this time P&W had been busy with major redesign to produce a greatly improved TF30 engine, and this finally matured as the JTF10A-32C, with military designation TF30-P-100. This was new from inlet to nozzle. The new fan and LP (low-pressure) compressor have a bulged inner profile, with backwards-canted blades at the front of the LP spool, removing flow-separation at the roots and dramatically improving tolerance of the engine to distorted flow in the inlet duct. The eight combustor cans are of a new Finwall pattern which are lighter, need only half as much cooling air, and give smokeless combustion with gas temperature raised to no less than 2,300deg F (1,260deg C), which is high even today.

To handle this increased temperature a completely new HP (high-pressure) turbine is fitted, with blades made from P&W's patented directionally cast process in which the metal crystals are aligned along the length of the blade, and with film-cooled stator vanes. Engine speeds are again increased, to a peak of 14,870rpm. And the afterburner is completely new, with five zones of combustion and a new electronic ignition system giving gentle 'soft-light' which reduces pressure excursions during light-up by almost 40 per cent compared with the previous fuel-squirt ignition. The nozzle is also quite new, with translating (rotary sliding) iris segments in the primary variable nozzle and a ring of 'tailfeathers' downstream which instead of being power-actuated are allowed to float to any position they assume.

The P-100 was such a tremendous improvement over all previous F-111 engines it really is a pity that "a constructive decision to stop production" could not have been taken until it was ready. It improved the takeoff thrust/weight ratio from 0·39 in the F-111A (hardly a 'fighter' type ratio!) to a more respectable 0·53 though even this is unimpressive compared with the figures of better than 1·0 for the F-15 and F-16. Sadly, the Air Force could not afford more than 106 of the final F-111 tactical model, the F-111F, nor could it retrofit the P-100 in any of the earlier aircraft.

P&W pressed on with TF30 improvement, and by 1970 had designed, and completed the underlying programme or research for, the next-generation engine designated JTF10A-39. Installationally interchangeable with the P-100, and actually lighter than any previous F-111 engine, this featured a modest increase in airflow and a further major jump in turbine temperature to 2,400deg F (1,316deg C), putting the engine in the 30,000lb (13,000kg) thrust class. The F-111 with this engine was calculated to have 5 per cent better rate of turn, 8 per cent faster climb after takeoff and 18 per cent faster supersonic acceleration, but the Air Force could not afford to buy the engine and instead terminated the F-111 programme.

Left: Not sixteen-inch guns but the overhauled P-3 engines being dollied back in to a newly converted EF in the Grumman Aerospace plant. The fuselage is tilted nose-down to bring the engine axes horizontal.

Avionics and Armament

To the media the One-Eleven is important because of its swing wing. In fact this is to a large degree incidental. What is central to its mission capability is a somewhat bulky and heavy array of electronic 'black boxes' which are described in this chapter. To be brutally frank, building these into any modern tactical aircraft would result in a much more effective interdiction attack system than one of today's One-Elevens with the avionics removed. Unfortunately the USAF ended up with a succession of One-Elevens with progressively better nav/attack systems but remarkably little commonality.

So far this book has discussed the F-111 purely as a flying machine. It is not to be forgotten that its purpose is to carry air-to-ground weapons and deliver them accurately to a target, or a heavy payload of EW (electronic-warfare) systems and operate them in precisely the correct place. And, to a degree surpassing that attained by any previous fighter-type aircraft, the F-111 has to fly these missions regardless of the time of day or the weather.

This chapter, therefore, deals with the basic on-board systems for navigation, flight control and weapon delivery, and with the added external devices for improved delivery accuracy or EW self-protection. The task is slightly complicated by the fact that the F-111 matured as a family of aircraft with several totally dissimilar avionic installations, which in turn results in each model having its own distinctive cockpit.

Indeed, whereas the need to introduce so many improved versions of the TF30 engine had never been considered, it had been half expected from early SOR-183 days that there might be

a case for progressive updating of the avionics. This is because, as a deliberate USAF policy, the basic F-111 had been planned around what might be called 'state of the art' black boxes, instead of the very latest solid-state digital technology. Thus, the avionics originally fitted were (and many still are) relatively bulky and heavy; and they consume a lot of electrical power, turning it into heat which has to be dissipated. Such penalties were willingly accepted in order to reap the expected large benefits of having hundreds, if not thousands, of F-111s all equipped with the same mature and reliable on-board systems fully meeting the tough numerical demands imposed by the customer in the matters of reliability and maintainability.

These demands, which were in many respects novel when written in 1960–61, were the most stringent that had been imposed at that time on any new aircraft. A few of them are the ability to: fly 30 hours per aircraft per month; move off within five minutes of an unpremeditated alert; take off within 30 minutes of

returning from the previous mission; demand not more than 35 man-hours per flight hour for all maintenance purposes; require no more than 15 minutes for identifying any fault in any system; require no more than 15 minutes for operational preflight checks; remain on continuous alert for five days; and be operationally ready 75 per cent of the time.

Thus, it was the original intention that the avionics should be in standardized modules, if possible one layer deep and with Bite (built-in test equipment) for rapid self-test and isolation of faults. Every area is covered by an easily opened door, almost all of which can be reached from ground level. Fundamentally the One-Eleven is a very superior aircraft in its design for maintainability, and the Air Force has only itself to blame for the increasingly troublesome situation in which no two wings fly the same version, and some wings have non-standard 'foreign' variants parked on the flightline.

In all versions the avionic fit is subdivided into three main groupings: fire-

Above: The USAF Rome Air Development Center (Systems Command) put the 15th RDT&E F-111A on a pedestal to measure avionics radiation patterns.

power control, penetration aids and MTC (mission and traffic control). The actual equipments installed are listed in the main data section. Apart from the progressive improvements in engine sub-type the avionics are the principal areas of difference between the five attack versions and one strategic version of the F-111. Avionics also include the flight-control system and instrumentation.

Flight control relies on the dual part-redundant and totally separated hydraulic systems and triplex (fully redundant) electronic autopilot. The system is self-adaptive, in that pilot input to the stick gives the same response at all aircraft speeds and altitudes and irres-

Below: A practice combat mission by the 474th TFW in the early days, with tandem triplets of Mk 83 bombs.

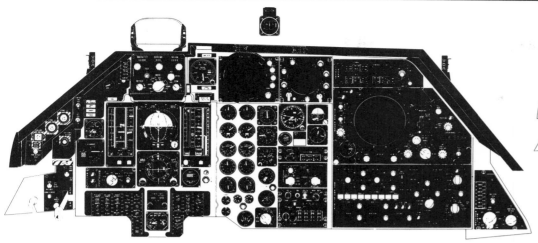

1 Engine fire pushbutton warning lamps
2 Fuselage fire pushbutton warning lamps
3 Agent discharge/Fire detect test switch
4 External stores jettison button
5 Landing gear control panel
6 ECM pod transmit control switches
7 Angle-of-attack indicator
8 Left warning and caution panel
9 Total temperature indicator
10 Wing sweep flap/slat position indicator
11 Upper warning and caution panel
12 Gun/camera control switch
13 Air-to-air IR missile switch
14 Instrument system coupler control panel
15 Landing gear position indicator lamps
16 Left main caution lamp panel
17 Lead computing optical sight and control panel
18 Upper warning and caution lamp panel
19 Integrated flight instruments
20 Dual bombing timer
21 Control surface position indicator
22 Nosewheel steering/Air refuelling indicator lamp
23 Radar altimeter
24 Stall warning lamp
25 Radar altitude low warning lamp
26 Master caution lamp
27 Bomb nav distance time indicator
28 Takeoff trim indicator lamp
29 Takeoff trim button
30 Right main caution lamp panel
31 Engine tachometers
32 Engine turbine inlet temperature indicator
33 Engine fuel flow indicators
34 Engine nozzle position indicators
35 Engine pressure ratio indicators
36 Engine oil pressure indicators
37 Hydraulic system pressure indicators
38 Oil quantity indicator test button
39 Oil quantity indicator
40 Air refuelling receptacle lights control knob
41 Fuselage fuel quantity indicator
42 Fuel quantity indicator test button
43 Total/Select fuel quantity indicator
44 Fuel quantity indicator selector knob
45 Terrain-following radar scope panel
46 Standby airspeed indicator
47 Bearing-distance-heading indicator
48 True airspeed indicator
49 Vertical velocity indicator
50 Clock
51 ECM threat panel
52 VHF radio control panel
53 TACAN control panel
54 Landing gear emergency release handle
55 Radar homing and warning scope panel
56 Standby attitude indicator
57 Standby altimeter
58 Radar homing and warning panel
59 Angle-of-attack indexer
60 Attack radar scope panel
61 Bomb nav control panel
62 Nuclear weapons control panel

Above: The F-111E has almost the same panel as the F-111A, though there are many small differences, and variations between aircraft.

pective of aircraft weight, within normal limits. In all attack and bomber versions both flight crew have sticks, and it is usual for the WSO in the right seat to 'get as much stick time as possible' as explained later.

The right side of the main instrument panel is normally occupied by radar and EW displays, flight instruments being in front of the pilot. The two central instruments (except in the D) comprise an ADI (attitude director indicator) above an HSI (horizontal situation indicator), flanked by four vertical tape instruments for Mach/airspeed (left) and altitude/VSI (vertical speed indicator) on the right. This region looks almost identical to that in GD's previous fighter, the F-106, and would be familiar to any USAF combat pilot. The rest of the front panel and the side consoles are another matter, and while they look impressive they would look archaic to anyone reared on GD's newest fighter, the F-16.

Certainly the oddest feature to an impartial observer is the wing sweep control. It is now over 40 years since designers began to shape vital cockpit controls in such a way that it became difficult to select the incorrect control, or move it in the wrong sense. For example, it became common to put a small wheel on the landing-gear retraction lever and a small flap on the flap lever. Yet, after extremely prolonged discussions, GD chose to make the vital wing-sweep actuator in the form of a sliding 'trombone lever' high on the left side, which bears no relation to the

wings and offers no instinctive guide as to which way it should be moved.

The extreme positions are indeed labelled AFT and FWD, but the fact remains at least three experienced pilots, one of them a company test pilot, have got it wrong and moved the lever the wrong way in low-level situations where the consequences were serious (the company accident was filled with ironies, not least being the tragic finale in which the uninjured copilot was sud-denly burned to death as he was helping the pilot to get out). One marvels that nobody insisted on having a small model One-Eleven on the left side with an easily gripped wing pivoting as in the actual aircraft.

Right top: The F-111A was the baseline aircraft. No two of the first 42 had identical cockpits. This diagram shows aircraft 103/159.

Right centre: The F-111D is so different that the most experienced driver of an A or E cannot even fly the D without a prolonged course of avionics instruction.

Right: Newest of the tactical models, the F-111F is a carefully judged compromise – but much better than a D crossed with an A! This panel shows today's F after the major installation of Pave Tack.

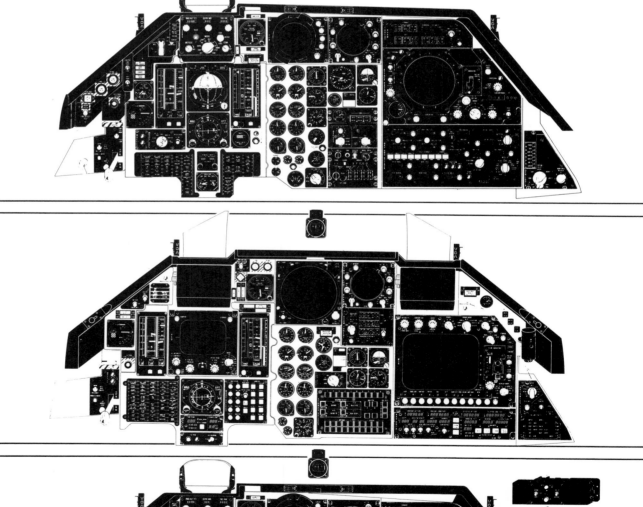

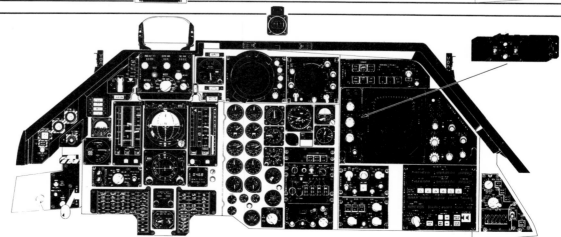

The original contractor for the attack radar was General Electric, whose APQ-113 is a hefty set operating in the J-band (formerly called Ku-band), and with its mechanically scanned antenna (aerial) enclosed in what must still be the biggest radome ever fitted to a fighter-type aircraft. This long nose was responsible for the unflattering popular name of Aardvark applied to the One-Eleven in 1968, which stuck to such a degree that today the EF version is the Spark Vark. The reflector dish is an unusual rounded-triangle shape to leave room underneath for the forward vision of the left/right dishes of the associated TFR (terrain-following radar), which was fitted to the F-111 for the first time in a production aircraft, though previously there had been terrain avoidance systems.

In the three main modes the APQ-113 scans 45deg left and right of either the aircraft centreline or the future track, and the depression angle (tilt) is adjusted either manually or automatically depending on the mode selected. Management is normally in the hands of the WSO, especially his right hand, which grips a short radar stick with which he can do several things, such as position cross-hairs directly over a ground target coming up ahead.

In the ground automatic mode the cross-hairs thenceforward are computer controlled, stay on target and feed back target azimuth (bearing) and exact range. In the ground velocity mode the target stays dead-centre in the radar scope, which thus shows only a small part of the total sweep of the radar, and is enlarged for greater precision in weapon delivery. There is an air-to-air mode which is compatible with the AIM-9 Sidewinder, which was often fired during early F-111A test flying, and which supplies range information to the pilot's LCOS (lead-computing optical sight). Picture resolution in the standard air-to-ground modes delighted the One-Eleven right-seaters when the F-111A was new, and is still considered perfectly acceptable today.

Terrain-following radar

Texas Instruments provided the F-111A with its vital APQ-110 TFR. Since the safety of the aircraft depends totally upon it when in the blind TF mode (at night or in bad weather), the whole system is duplicated, with dual signal channels to two small scanners which look ahead and, via a computerized link to the autopilot, automatically command the aircraft to follow the land contours when the TF mode is selected.

Obviously, flying over a flat desert the TFR might see high mountains many miles ahead, and as the objective is to stay as low as possible 'under the enemy radar' it would be foolish if it at once commanded a pull up to climb over the mountains. Accordingly, the APQ-110 is designed according to the 'adaptive angle' principle, which was pioneered in Britain and by workers at the Cornell Aeronautical Laboratory. This automatically injects a 'depressing function' into the TFR to stop it from commanding a climb. As the range to the mountain decreases, so does the depressing function wind down to zero at the minimum safe distance. Then the climb command reaches the autopilot, and the Aardvark nose at last lifts as if the aircraft was being cushioned against the rock slope just in front.

Additional shaping of the electronic signals ensures that, as the F-111 flashes over the top of the mountain ridge it is already in level flight as it reaches the top, instead of being catapulted into radar-infested space. Likewise, the instant it breasts the summit the nose

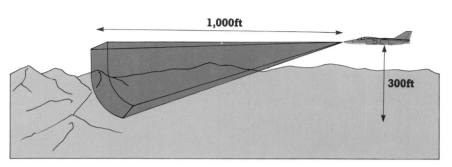

Top: Texas Instruments supplied the APQ-146 terrain-following radar used in the F-111F and as a retrofit in older models. Note duplicate system but single control box and display.

pitches sharply down (unless there is another peak ahead within the minimum safe distance) to keep the aircraft descending as close as possible to the back side of the mountain until it reaches the valley floor beyond.

Technicians call this a ski-toe locus, because the aircraft flies as if it was riding on a ski with an upturned toe in front. It does not rise over an obstruction until the (frighteningly short) ski toe reaches it. It ignores all obstructions ahead until they come within range. And a little thought will show, first, that the TFR has to take account of obstructions to left and right of track (because the pilot may alter course suddenly) and, second, that in a banked turn at low level it must continue to record the true height above ground and not the increased distance measured to the ground along the aircraft's own vertical axis.

An analog computer continuously calculates which of perhaps many nearby obstacles should be the one to control the flight trajectory, and in some situations (meeting a thousand-foot TV mast, for example) to indicate that it is better to go around than over. Throughout TF flight the APQ-110 automatically subjects itself to a gross performance check every 0·7 second; if it fails to pass one of these tests it automatically commands a changeover within 0·3 second to the

Above: In TF mode the F-111 can fly at 300ft (90m) AGL. The radar scans 1,000ft ahead, commanding a pull-up manoeuvre should an obstacle be detected.

alternative TFR. Should this fail it commands a 2g pull-up manoeuvre and blinks a bright warning to the crew.

During TF flight only one of the APG-110 radars commands the aircraft; the other can be used to give a terrain-avoidance display to assist the pilot to take decisions on weaving his way through high ground ahead and to monitor the performance of the TF system, or it can even operate in a lateral (sideways) scan mode as a backup mapping and navigation radar. The pilot can select a soft, medium or hard ride, depending on how essential it is to follow the terrain contours, and dial in any height AGL down to a normal minimum of 200ft (61m) AGL.

Low-level flight

In the manual mode it is not unknown for pilots to demonstrate high speeds at 100ft (30m) AGL in favourable circumstances, and it is also possible in full after-burner to reach Mach 1·2 with a clean aircraft at minimum TF height, which in desert areas kicks up the dust so that the aircraft's progress looks from a distance exactly like an endless stick of bombs exploding. At all times the radar altimeter (APN-167 in the F-111A) monitors clearance between the aircraft and the ground and, should this fall below a preseleted minimum, this too can trigger a 2g pull-up and signal a

simultaneous visual warning to the crew.

In all TF modes the crew can monitor progress with a visual TFR display at the top centre of the instrument panel where it can be clearly seen by both crew. Once tuned it displays two thin green lines, the lower one the irregular outline of the terrain ahead and the upper one the profile the aircraft will follow. There are many intriguing facets to TF flight, one being that, at the end of the hi (40,000ft (12,000m) or thereabouts) outbound cruise part of a mission the aircraft is pushed over into a dive automatically by switching on the TF mode. The pilot's and WSO's sticks do not move; the aircraft slides downhill guided by other hands. At about 5,000ft (1,500m) AGL the radar altimeter picks up the terrain below and, still without the sticks moving, the dive steepens perceptibly until the TFR ski-toe touches bottom and a smooth pull-out is commanded into the helter-skelter of TF flight. To anyone not used to it TF flight is terrifying, and among mountains in cloud or at night it is doubtful that anyone can avoid a considerable increase in pulse-rate!

Another subsystem in the firepower control is the NAS (nav/attack set), the chief element of which is the Litton AJQ-20A inertial bomb/nav system. Like any INS (inertial navigation system) it is totally independent of weather or any other external influence, though for proper accuracy the aircraft parking spots on the ramp have to be precisely surveyed so that the starting point of the mission is known.

The complete NAS, with a BCU (ballistics computer unit) not only guides the aircraft in three dimensions but also collaborates with the main attack radar to provide an automatic radar bombing capability. Iron bombs can be delivered by the WSO punching the button to recall the target co-ordinates inserted into the BCU before departure, which makes the cross-hairs on the main radar display automatically align themselves with the approaching target. The BCU automatically adjusts itself for changes in aircraft trajectory, including height (which constantly varies under TFR command) and speed. It is also possible to bomb manually using standard ballistics for the bombs inserted before takeoff and aiming through the LCOS, with release commanded by the 'pickle button' under the pilot's right thumb. Yet another capability of the NAS is to give the F-111 a self-contained blind-letdown and ILS (instrument landing system) ability, even to a runway without radar, ILS or even radio. The main ILS steering information is displayed on the LCOS.

CNI equipment

CNI (communications, navigation and identification) facilities are grouped in the mission & traffic group, which in fact does include an ILS (ARN-58). Other equipment includes Singer GPL doppler radar, ARN-52 Tacan, ARA-50 UHF/DF and a comprehensive fit of communications radios including HF, UHF and interphone. The usual IFF interrogator is the APX-64 AIMS (aircraft identification monitoring system).

This leads into the vital question of penaids (penetration aids), which complement the firepower control in enabling the F-111 to fulfil its mission. Obviously the USAF wished this aircraft to set an entirely new level of sophistication in EW (electronic warfare) equipment. Though it was clear that external jammer pods would be needed the F-111 was certainly the first tactical jet to have an internal ECM system, and the first with RHAWS fitted

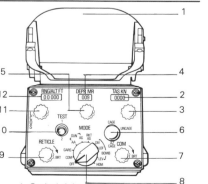

1 Weapon release button
2 Trim button
3 Reference engage button
4 Aerial refuel and nose
  wheel steering button
5 Gun trigger
6 Autopilot release lever

Above: The top of the pilot's control stick contains the expected weapon release and other controls. Right: The LCOS is fitted with variations in the earlier tactical models.

1 Optical sight
2 Preset IAS indicator
3 IAS set knob
4 Reticle depression indictor
5 Reticle depression set knob
6 Aiming reticle cage lever
7 Command bar brightness knob
8 Mode select knob
9 Aiming reticle brightness knob
10 Test switch
11 Pitch degree set knob
12 Pitch degree indicator

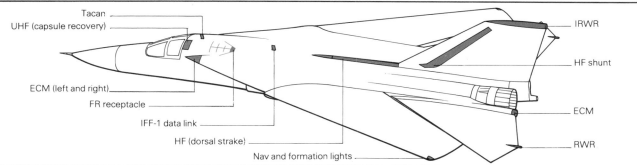

AAM or hostile fighter. Avco supplied the original ECM receiver subsystem, though the Transco ALR-4 was one early fit.

Like the Elint (electronic intelligence) passive receivers just described, the offensive ECM have varied greatly from one F-111 version to another, and also because of progressive updating. The F-111 could have been modified to house internal jammers and dispensing systems, but the objections were time, cost, supposed inflexibility of a built-in system, difficulty of getting good all-round coverage and the penalty of always having an item installed that usually (in peacetime) would not be needed. Even today there is much argument, and external pods remain the favoured answer. The chief contractor for dispensed payloads was originally Lundy, with the ALE-28, and the same company has later supplied the ALE-44. Both are mounted upstream of the rear ECM aerials, inboard of the tailerons, and dispense chaff or flares. The WSO controls the operation from a panel at upper right which shows the number of payloads of each type remaining, and provides for selection of burst rates, burst intervals and payload units per burst.

The F-111 pioneered internal ECM systems in slender fighter-type aircraft, in the Western world at least, though details of where the boxes are installed have not been made public. The original system designed for the F-111 was the ALQ-94, by Sanders Associates, a company previously a supplier of EW equipment for Navy aircraft. A reported 500-plus sets were delivered, each providing both noise and deception jamming along dual channels and with a CW (continuous-wave) capability which certainly antedated the 'shock discovery' in the Yom Kippur war in 1973 that no Israeli or US ECM was effective against the SA-6 SAM. Today the -94 is being replaced by the -137, as noted later.

External ECM pods

A major objection to external jammer pods is that they not only add drag but they occupy pylons, but in the F-111 this is much less important because the pod pylons are under the fuselage and cannot be used for dropped stores such as bombs. In the early years of the F-111 the standard ECM pod was the General Electric ALQ-87, a modest pod yet considerably better than those available in the mid-1960s. On entering service in partnership with the F-111A in 1967 the ALQ-87, previously called the ORC-160-8 from its ancestry in the prolonged ORC-160 research programme, was intended to be an effective barrage jammer against both surface threats and interceptor radars. Using a backward-wave oscillator it was extended to cover G/H (previously C) band followed by I/J (previously X and Ku) bands by the time it went to Vietnam in 1968. A year later it was further extended into the shorter wavelengths in the upper J band. Its electric power is generated by a self-contained ram-air windmill, and a distinctive recognition feature is the pair of ventral blade aerials.

Usually two ALQ-87s were carried in tandem on the widely separated racks under the internal bomb bay and between the rear ventral strakes. Subsequently the widely used Westinghouse ALQ-101 pod was also used. Stemming from the QRC-335 programme, these pods are available in several versions, some (notably the ALQ-101(V)8, deployed in large numbers) having a ventral gondola to give an approximately doubled spread of frequencies covered. Unlike the GE pod this family

Top: Newest of the ECM pods carried by tactical One-Elevens, the ALQ-131(V) is the latest mass-production type of the Westinghouse company.

Above: Simplified key to some of the external avionics aerials (antennae) of an F-111A.

Left: Tail of an F-111F of the 48th TFW (the wing commander's aircraft) showing the tip pod, low-voltage formation light (pale cream strip) and blunt-ended ECM emitter.

Left below: Close-up of an F-111F showing the left ECM transmitter.

from the very start, and it was also probably the first to have an internal integrated warning system for all radar and IR (infra-red) wavelengths.

The initial RHAWS (radar homing and warning system) was the Dalmo-Victor APS-109 and 109A, with the main miniature spiral receiver aerials in pointed pods facing astern from the rearmost points of the tailplanes and the side-looking aerials beneath glassfibre panels which made a prominent and distinctive pattern on each side of the nose until, from about 1978, they began to be painted over. The cockpit display, surrounded by no fewer than nine control knobs, is at the top right of the panel immediately to the right of the TFR scope.

The original IRWR (IR warning receiver) was the Cincinnati Electronics AAR-34 backed up by the same suppliers ALR-23, of which some 700 pairs were supplied for the F-111 programme. These are tuned to warn of the approach of any burning hydrocarbon gas such as would trail behind a SAM,

Top: A gun-equipped F-111D of the 27th TFW at Cannon AFB. Proposals still exist to rebuild this model into SAC bombers.

Above: The strike camera installation of an F-111D, typical of most tactical models. It looks obliquely forward but the outer window is skin-flush.

have no windmill, but have hemispherical radomes emitting to front and rear.

This overall avionic fit was retained with only very minor changes in the second production version, the F-111E. The RAAF virtually accepted the entire Mk I avionics for the F-111C, though this has a modified airframe, as explained in a later chapter. But as early as 1963 the USAF Systems Command had begun detailed investigation of a Mk II avionics fit, and though this may be fractured English it eventually came to describe a totally new aircraft, but packaged inside virtually the same airframe as the A and E models. The reason was simply that by the mid-1960s the Mk I black boxes had begun to look distinctly dated, with analog technology, large printed-circuit boards often bearing discrete components, and a general level of technology hardly different from an F-4. Clearly, it was possible to do much better with more modern technology, and it looked as if the F-111 could be transformed into a virtually new-generation aircraft.

By 1964 the Mk II avionics specification and equipment list had been agreed, and the prime contract for systems integration was placed with North American Aviation's Autonetics Division, today called Rockwell International Electronics. Some parts of mission/traffic control and penaids were left alone, but the central firepower control and associated cockpit displays were virtually designed from a clean sheet of paper.

It was planned to switch to the Mk II at the 100th production F-111 in 1968, the new model being designated F-111D. What actually happened was that

the exciting new Mk II system – which at one time the British government thought it could have in the RAF in 1968 also – took so long to develop that costs multiplied frighteningly, delays became severe and eventually it went into a mere 96 aircraft, compared with a planned 315. Even so, major elements of the Mk II system were omitted, one being CW illumination for AIM-7 Sparrow AAMs to restore some capability in the air-to-air mission.

Largest item in the firepower control is the attack radar, and in the Mk II system this is the Autonetics APQ-130. Essentially the next generation after the same company's ASB-12 (REINS) radar bombing system for the A-5 Vigilante, APQ-130 is a digital solid-state device with more operating modes than the APQ-113. It can offer considerably improved picture sharpness in ground map modes, especially at the very shallow grazing angles of tree-top TF flight, offers MTI (moving-target indication) in being able to pick out a moving target against a stationary surface background, and in particular has vastly improved performance in conditions of heavy precipitation (rain or snow) or enemy countermeasures.

In the early days of the F-111 WSOs who came from older aircraft would not allow that there could ever be a better radar than the APQ-113 but the 130 is a new-generation set with many capabilities not dissimilar to the F-15's APG-63 and Tornado's TI attack radar. In theory such a radar needs less cooling and is far more reliable than older sets, but in practice the abort rate of the F-111D has generally been worse than that of all

other variants, largely because of problems with the temperamental avionics.

Other items making up the Mk II suite are listed in the detailed data section.

Below: The Pave Tack pod is normally housed inside the weapon bay. As the target approaches it is quickly extended (Mach limit is 1.4) and pointed within the limits shown.

Supplier of the APQ-128 TFR is Sperry, the APN-189 doppler comes from Canadian Marconi, GD and IBM produced the totally new general-purpose digital computer, and in the cockpit the D has a very advanced HSD (Astronautics Corp AYN-3) which superimposes aircraft position, track and target data over projected maps or reconnaissance photographs, while directly ahead of

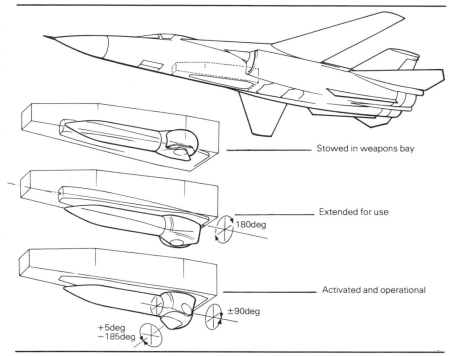

Stowed in weapons bay

Extended for use 180deg

Activated and operational ±90deg +5deg −185deg

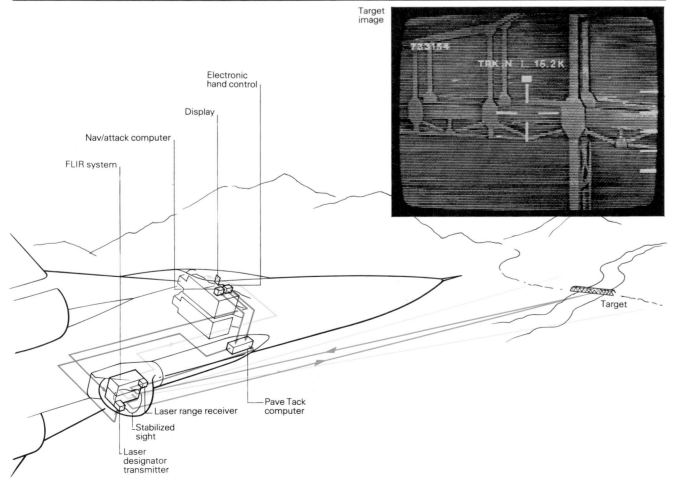

Target image

Above: Pave Tack became operational on 15 September 1981 with F-111Fs of the 48th TFW at RAF Lakenheath. This F-111F is carrying a 2,450lb (1,111kg) GBU-15.

Left: Simplified Pave Tack functional diagram, with an inset video image (in this case of a bridge target).

both crew members is an AVA-9 HUD, by Norden Division of what is today called United Technologies, one of the first head-up displays in the USAF and a major cause of Mk II delays and problems. In the centre of the pilot's panel is a VSD (vertical situation display) almost as impressive as the giant HSD on the right, and more than half the other cockpit items look different from those in the A and E versions.

As noted earlier the D introduced a more powerful TF30 engine, and a more important advance was the introduction of a 'bootstrap-cycle' ECS (environmental control system), though this was yet another cause of severe technical problems. One of the few changes in the D that showed externally was the replacement of the often-criticized manually operated scope camera, used for photographing targets, by a KB-18A automatic strike camera. This looks obliquely ahead from a small blister under the forward fuselage, and has been retrofitted on most F-111As and Es, in some cases after relocation of an ALE-23 or ALR-41 blade aerial.

Left: Trials with the Hughes version of Pave Mover have been flown with this F-111E, mainly at White Sands Missile Range, New Mexico. The radar components and data link ride in the large underbelly pod.

Left below: The Pave Mover data link sends the radar target information to a mobile ground station to create this full-colour battlefield display. Computers display the alphanumeric data on all significant targets.

Left bottom: An F-111D lets go 12 Mk 82 bombs over Nevada in July 1972.

Altogether the F-111D is unquestionably a superior aircraft, and one with a bit more accent on air combat, a facet also shown by the invariable installation of the gun, as described in the next chapter. But the CW illumination of air targets for Sparrow AAMs has never been used, and there is no plan to fit either these weapons or the later Amraam. On balance, therefore, the D remains a questionable programme, which has absorbed very large sums of money, given relatively poor mission availability and required the training of flight and ground crews who cannot operate or maintain other F-111s.

The situation would have been better had the D become the standard model; indeed, there was even discussion in the 1964–5 period of retrofitting the Mk II avionics to the F-111A. Cost proved to be prohibitive, and the Mk II research bill alone escalated from a projected $60 million to more than $280 million by 1969. At quite a late stage the decision was taken to go ahead with the planned fitment of larger mainwheel tyres and a stronger landing gear, but the increase in gross weight thus permitted was minimal, and in fact seldom used. The D had also been planned as the standard photo and multisensor reconnaissance model, designated RF-111D.

The original idea was that TAC would buy large pallets carrying optical cameras, a SLAR (side-looking airborne radar) and IR linescan, and clip them into the weapon bays of regular F-111As. It was found difficult to do this, and in December 1967 the 11th development aircraft (63-9776) began a flight programme as the RF-111A, with a multisensor installation which was not readily removable. Over $118 million was spent on the RF system, and as late as 1968 it was hoped to buy 60 RF-111Ds with a similar installation, managed by a separate digital computer, but the RF programme was cancelled. This left the RAAF later to spend a lot more money on a quite different RF-111C programme of its own.

Final tactical version

Chronologically the next variant was the FB-111A, discussed in a later chapter. The tactical models were completed with the F-111F, and had it not been for Pratt & Whitney it is doubtful that this model would ever have been purchased. Though the earlier One-Elevens can do their job, and in *Airman Magazine* for August 1969, the most experienced of all F-111 pilots, Maj Tom Wheeler (USAF Chief of Flight Test and Acceptance at GD), wrote "The power plant on this bird is so good that you can do a lot of flying on one engine", the fact remains the thrust/weight ratio of the fully loaded aircraft was unimpressive even for a bomber, and about one-third as high as modern fighters. There was certainly an urge to counter the unplanned and awesome increase in gross weight with additional engine thrust, but it took a long time to do this, in part because P&W were busy getting the

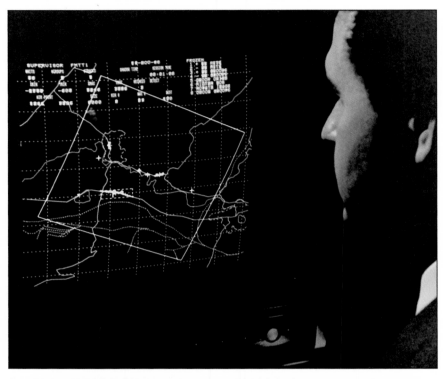

engine to an acceptable standard of reliability when installed in the F-111A. As noted earlier they finally came up with the P-100 engine offering a welcome 35 per cent more power than the F-111A and E engines, and with other big advantages, and this tipped the scales in favour of a planned buy of 219 of the F version.

Ideally these should otherwise have had the standard Mk II avionics to maximise both capability and commonality, but the mixture of technical problems and astronomic costs spurred a search for a more affordable alternative. This was realised in the Mk IIB system (a designation originally applied to the FB-111A avionics), which were considered the best compromise between capability and price. Officially said to cost just half as much as the Mk II system, the IIB has the AYK-6 digital computer from the Mk II but used to tie together generally simplified black boxes and with a cockpit much more familiar to a driver of an A or E.

New Mk IIB avionics

The attack radar is the APG-144, based on the GE radar of the FB-111A but with the addition of 0·2-microsecond pulsewidth (half the previous minimum) and a 2½nm (4·63km) display scale, again half the previous minimum and giving double the 'magnification'. GE wished to add DMTI (digital moving-target indication) and a reduced wavelength in the K-band, but though these were flown they were never incorporated in production sets. (Later the same radar formed the basis of those used in prototype B-1 bombers.) Another new item was the Loral ALR-41 CMRS (countermeasures receiver set), but by 1980 this was being replaced by the new-generation Dalmo-Victor ALR-62 as part of the USAF's across-the-board efforts to update the EW suites of all F-111s. The ALR-62 RWR is now the chief sensor in the updated F-111 kit for the remainder of the 1980s, which also includes the AAR-44 and ALQ-137.

Though still partly classified, the AAR-44 is the latest in a series of IRWRs (infra-red warning receivers) by Cincinnati Electronics, and it retains the fin-top location of the receiver cells – which, of course, are refrigerated by a cryogenic system. This installation can continue its non-stop search of the entire hemisphere below the aircraft whilst locking-on and tracking any oncoming SAM or AAM and processing the resulting data for display to the crew. IRCM (countermeasure) action can be automatic, in other words the AAR-44 can itself trigger the release of flare cartridges from the ALE-28 installation at the optimum times and with the best frequency and burst characteristics to protect the aircraft without the crew having to work out the answers under extreme stress. The system can handle attacks by several missiles simultaneously, and is claimed to have near-perfect ability to discriminate true targets against solar radiation or the

Sun's reflection on glass or water, and known kinds of IRCM background.

ALQ-137 is an internal EW system developed specially for the F-111 family as a replacement for the same company's ALQ-94. The 137 may be expected to have higher ERP (effective radiated power) and will certainly have more advanced digital processing to manage the electric power for the maximum result, with either or both noise and deception signals being sent out not to all points of the compass but towards the threat being countered. Trials began in 1974 and the first production contract was placed in 1977, the installation being integrally linked with the ALR-62 to form the first really modern

Above: An F-111A with 24 Mk 82 bombs operating with the 366th TFW.

Right: Standard MER (multiple ejector rack) of the kind carried by F-111s for conventional bombing.

Below: An F-111A of the 474th TFW on Constant Guard Five deployment to Southeast Asia in December 1972. It is shown on a combat mission from Takhli RTAFB loaded with CBU-42 cluster bombs.

Foot of page: An unidentified F-111A photographed in 1971 with a display showing the number carried of each store (white bombs are nuclear).

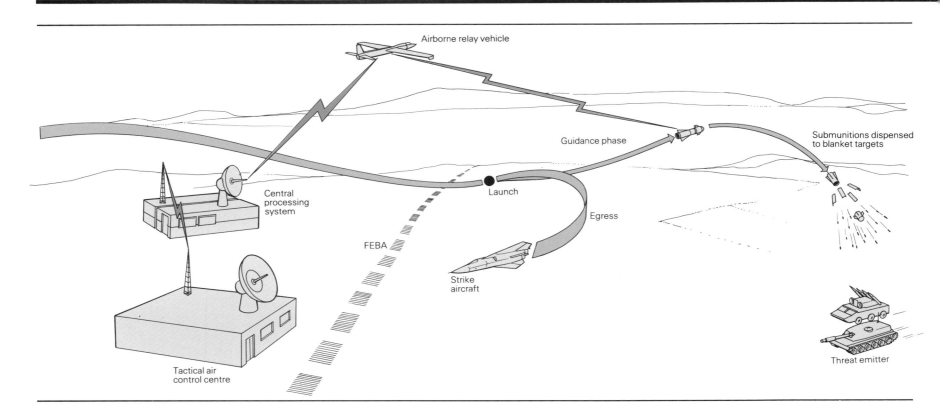

Airborne relay vehicle

Guidance phase

Submunitions dispensed to blanket targets

Central processing system

Launch

Egress

FEBA

Strike aircraft

Tactical air control centre

Threat emitter

EW package in any tactical aircraft. Of course, it is likely that by the mid-1980s the ITT/Westinghouse ALQ-165 ASPJ (advanced self-protective jammer) will be installed in the surviving F-111s, as well as in all front-line combat aircraft of the USAF, Navy and Marines. This extremely advanced installation is intended to be internal in all aircraft, and to counter threats at frequencies up to 20 GHz from the start, 35 GHz by about 1989 and perhaps 140 GHz by the end of the century, given the expected improvements in capabilities.

New Avionics
Remarkably, in view of the extremely comprehensive internal fit of sensors and weapon-delivery systems, the F-111 has in recent years been a favoured vehicle for extra avionics in these categories. As far as combat effectiveness is concerned, by far the most important of the add-ons is AVQ-26 Pave Tack, one of the many 'Pave' projects initiated by USAF Aeronautical Systems Division. It is briefly described as a versatile target designator for use at all times of day and in all kinds of weather. Prime contractor is Ford Aerospace but key elements include a FLIR by TI, a laser by International Laser Systems and a virtual image display by GE. Flying in an F-111F began in August 1978, the sensor pod being mounted on a cradle which extends it upon command from its normal retracted position in the weapon bay. When extended the sensor head can view the entire hemisphere beneath the aircraft.

The pod comprises a streamlined tubular Base Unit packed with elec-

Above: The Advanced Location/Strike System uses TOA (time of arrival of radar pulses) and DME (distance measuring equipment) to hit enemy radars with GBU-15s.

Below: A fine January 1983 portrait of one of the 48th TFW's F-111Fs with Pave Tack and four Paveway IIs.

tronics, digital computer and refrigeration, and a spherical Head Unit able to be rotated at high speed and with great precision to look in any direction. The

Above: Though the F-111 has always been nominally a 'fighter', and early prototypes were cleared with the AIM-9 Sidewinder, it is only very recently that such self-defence AAMs have appeared in use. This bombed-up F-111F shows the neat way that AIM-9 is carried on the side of the pylon.

Right: The fourth F-111B Navy fighter flying with four dummy AIM-54 Phoenix long-range AAMs. The same powerful air-to-air interception weapons were also flown on the fourth USAF F-111A RDT&E aircraft, but no attempt was subsequently made to give USAF F-111s stand-off interception capability.

Head contains the AAQ-9 FLIR and AVQ-25 YAG (yttrium/aluminium garnet) laser, both boresighted exactly parallel to a precision-stabilized optical sight. All sensors are isolated from vibration, and look through a large window of ZnS (zinc sulphide). The FLIR provides a ×1 or ×2 video picture of a narrow 3deg or wide 12deg field of view on 525 or 875 lines, on which can be superimposed the bright reticle of the laser designator and a great variety of alphanumeric information. The line of sight may be aimed by a hand control-

ler or controlled automatically by various systems.

Once the target is being tracked it remains in the display no matter what evasive manoeuvres are performed, and while the sightline gives exact angle information the laser gives range information, within much less than 10ft (3m), for precision weapon delivery. The laser emits at 1·06 microns and is thus compatible with Paveway-series and other smart weapons. The head swivels aft to give damage information on leaving the target, everything if

necessary being taped for subsequent playback.

The display was accommodated by taking the space previously occupied by the APQ-144 (main radar) indicator/recorder system. Funding limitations have restricted Pave Tack buy for F-111Fs to a mere 49 pods, though all active aircraft are being converted to take them. Operational clearance with the 48th TFW was reached in 1981, since when the training burden has been considerable. Pave Tack has also been purchased for RAAF F-111Cs.

Another Pave system not yet cleared for use on any aircraft is Pave Mover. This ambitious TAWDS (target acquisition/weapon delivery system) is based on an SAR (synthetic-aperture radar) which, as described earlier in this book, emits sequenced signals as if from a giant antenna to give very high resolution. Two Pave Mover SARs are flying in F-111s, a Hughes in an F-111E and a joint Norden/Grumman in an F-111A. Norden/Grumman was the team on the A-6 Intruder for the US Navy, and their Pave Mover was based on work done in

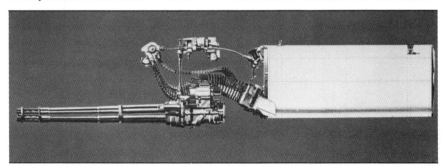

Top: The M61A-1 gun installation includes the biggest ammunition tank ever fitted to any fighter, with a capacity of up to 2,084 20mm rounds.

Above: The box containing the M61 gun seen installed but with the weapon bay doors open. The gun is on the right side, with muzzles to the left.

Right: The gun in an F-111F of the 366th TFW, showing the muzzle fairing carried to reduce drag.

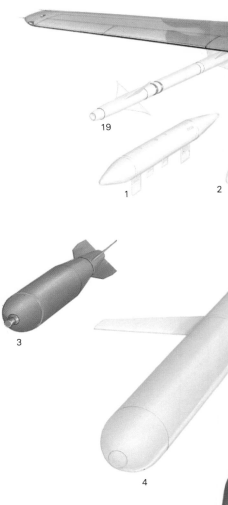

Key to stores

1. ALQ-87 jammer pod (being withdrawn)
2. ALQ-131 jammer pod (entering service)
3. Mk 117 750lb (340kg) GP bomb
4. AGM-109 MRASM cruise missile
5. Twin bomb dispensers
6. Stores container
7. Mk 82 Snakeye retarded bomb
8. AGM-69A SRAM (FB-111A only)
9. M61 20mm cannon
10. B61 nuclear weapon
11. Nuclear weapon (type undisclosed, possibly B28 carried by FB-111A)
12. Mk 83 1,000lb (454kg) GP bomb
13. 600US gal drop tank
14. GBU-15 laser-guided bomb
15. B43 nuclear weapon
16. Mk 84 2,000lb (907kg) GP bomb
17. ALQ-119(V) ECM jammer pod
18. Durandal anti-runway weapon
19. AIM-9L Sidewinder AAM

updating that programme. The Norden/Grumman set is long and slim and required extensive aircraft modification but is mounted on a quickly removed pallet and gives little drag. The Hughes radar is fatter and mounted largely external below the weapon bay, needing modest aircraft modification but imposing higher drag. Both are SLARs (side-looking aircraft radars) working in I/J band with aerial arrays 11·5ft (3·5m) long, and both use the latest combinations of frequency hopping, spread spectrum PRN (pseudo-random noise) techniques to make it very difficult for enemy ECM to get a good lock or determine their direction or range. This is vital, because the carrier aircraft would be the first thing to be destroyed and extremely vulnerable, orbiting at about 49,000ft (15km) for long periods and playing a crucial role in directing air attack on the enemy.

Pave Mover has been used mainly in connection with the USAF Assault Breaker concept for stopping a thrust by vast forces of armoured vehicles. Attacks could be made by manned aircraft, such as normal F-111s, or by missiles with single warheads or missiles with dispensed submunitions with or without individual guidance. All these, including even the unguided submunitions, could benefit from Pave Mover surveillance, which gives a pinsharp picture of stationary objects on the battlefield and also can detect and track moving objects.

The radars flying in the two F-111s can each detect and track six separate "target arrays" each comprising up to 12 objects such as tanks, whilst simultaneously transmitting target guidance updates to two missiles or aircraft. Trials from Holloman AFB began in June 1981 and in 1983 decisions on the next stage

were expected. There are problems with C³ – command, control, communications – and with discriminating between high-value tanks and SP guns and low-value targets or even decoys. Moreover, there is never enough money to progress in the way needed to stay even abreast of the threat on the European Central Front.

Yet another F-111 add-on is the AXQ-14 data-link which rather surprisingly is needed to allow GBU-15 missiles to be guided effectively. Though GBU-15 is a Rockwell weapon, also known as CWW (cruciform-wing weapon), the data-link is a Hughes Aircraft product, and it is hung on the rear fuselage, displacing the ECM jammer pod to a new location under the weapon bay. In the photograph a full-size F-111 mock-up is mounted upside-down to avoid ground interference while the data-link is tested at full power (with an ALQ-119 jammer further forward). The AXQ-14 emits from a phased-array aerial system to guide the missile into its target, whilst at the same time relaying the image seen by the missile's EO nose seeker to the F-111 cockpit display. The pod also includes the usual mission recorder.

Weapons for the One-eleven

As the original concept of SOR-183 was an aircraft to replace the F-105 it is not surprising that the F-111 ended up with plenty of pylon capacity, an internal weapon bay and a 20-mm M61 'Gatling gun'. At the same time, in view of the extremely high price of so large and complex an aircraft, and the desire to fly fighter missions, and perhaps enjoy commonality with the Navy air-dfence fighter, it is a little surprising that weapons for the air-combat and interception roles appear to have been almost overlooked.

Dealing with this mission first, several early development aircraft were used in flight test programmes with AAMs. The No 7 aircraft (63-9772) was fitted with a remarkably complex system of twin staggered pairs of rails for launching Sidewinder close-range AAMs. Each pair of rails was hung on parallel links from the top of the weapon bay and with the bay doors open could pivot down to place the missiles out in the airstream well below the fuselage. This fit was not adopted, though on all tactical versions Pylons 3,4,5 and 6 can have shoes for launching any model of AIM-9 Sidewinder (though they are almost never carried).

The No 4 aircraft (63-9769) was flown with dummy AIM-54 Phoenix AAMS on the four inboard wing pylons (Nos 3, 4, 5 and 6). This large and extremely long-ranged AAM was to have been the primary armament of the F-111B, and its great performance was naturally of interest to the USAF, though the associated AWG-9 radar could not handle parts of the Air Force attack mission. Predictably, the more the F-111 became a bomber, the less the USAF thought about Phoenix. Unlike Sidewinder, Phoenix was never actually fired from any Air Force version of F-111.

The wish to add the AIM-7 Sparrow medium-range AAM to the weapon kit of the F-111 has already been related. The MK II avionics suite was specially designed so that the main attack radar would have an AAM mode in which it could provide a CW pencil beam to illuminate a hostile aircraft. This mode is not used, and no Sparrow ever flew on an F-111, though should this capability be thought important it could fairly readily be provided.

As it is, the gun is today the only part of the regular weapon fit regarded as an

air-to-air weapon, and it is not normally carried except by the F-111D and occasionally by other models. Except for the 27th TFW, most One-Eleven crews have never even seen it, far less fired it. The installation is not unusual, the gun being mounted on the right centre of the forward part of the bomb bay, faired inside a blister built into the right-hand bay door which is provided with a removable front fairing. The door and fairing can be swung open for access to the gun. A round-trip flexible guideway feeds ammunition from the enormous 2,084-round drum in the rear of the bay, to which empty cases are returned. The gun is aimed with the pilot's LCOS (or HUD in the F-111D) and is considered useful against certain ground targets.

When the gun is not installed, the bomb bay can be used for various purposes including carriage of ECM dispensers (for bulk chaff in particular), fuel and/or water tanks, special instrumentation, and, in the RF-111C, a reconnaissance installation. The brochures say that two 750lb (340kg) bombs can be carried in the bay, but in fact the standard USAF stores loadings

Below: a selection of stores carried by the F-111 (the aircraft is typical of all tactical attack versions).

Below: a selection of stores carried by the F-111 (the aircraft is typical of all tactical attack versions).

do not include any internal items except nuclear bombs, practice bombs and the gun.

Standard nuclear bombs which can be carried by the F-111 include the B43, B57 and B61, all in tactical versions and the former with at least five different yields. In each case one bomb can be carried in both the left and right bays. When the gun is carried only the right bay is fully occupied but none of these weapons can be carried on the left side. As noted later, the FB-111A can carry two SRAMS, internally; AGM-86B ALCM cannot be accommodated.

The only fuselage pylons are for ECM pods, and for practical purposes the only armament is what can be carried on the wing pylons. The outer wings have four hardpoints on each side, and weapon loads have been published which require eight pylons, but though these were flown during early test programmes they are not used in practice, and the outermost pylons, Nos 1 and 8, positioned at BL (buttock-line) 309 (ie, 309 in or 25ft 9in [7·85m] from the aircraft centreline) are not fitted.

This leaves a maximum capacity of six pylons. The outers, Nos 2 and 7, each at BL 250, are fixed to the wing at such an angle that they are aligned with the fore/aft axis only when the wings are at the 26deg sweep position. In theory it would be possible to take off with the wings fully forward with these pylons installed, though it is certainly not normal practice. At any sweep angle greater than 26deg these pylons must be jettisoned. The only load normally carried on these pylons is the 600US gal (500gal, 2,273-litre) drop tank.

Thus in practice there are just four pylons available for conventional weapons: Nos 3,4,5 and 6, located at BL 189 and 118 on each side of the aircraft. These pylons are the only ones normally installed, and they were the first in the world to be mounted on pivots with internal linkage to keep them aligned with the airstream at all wing sweep angles. All are stressed to 5,000lb (2,268kg) to 4·6g, the heaviest load being the 600US gal tank which weighs almost this amount when filled. Other possible loads are listed in the data. Normal maximum bombload is thus 19,800lb (8,981kg), comprising 24 M117A1 GP bombs each of 750lb nominal weight but an actual weight nearer to 825lb (374kg).

Nuclear bombs, such as B43, B57 and B61, the Mk 84 family of 2,000lb (907kg) bombs and the M118 bomb of 3,000lb (1,361kg) nominal mass are all carried singly. Other stores are carried in multiple, either four or six to each of the four pylons. This requires the addition of an MER (multiple ejector rack) to each pylon. The F-111 has its own unique design of MER which, while preserving

the usual basically triangular section, has a waisted centre and a bulged front and rear, with ventral strakes, giving it an area-ruled appearance. It carries all stores in tandem triplets, the heaviest load of six CBU-58s (cluster bomb units, each housing 800 bomblets of 1lb) having roughly the same aggregate mass as the 600US gal tank.

There is no reason to doubt that Maverick could be carried in tandem triplets, but this is not a certified F-111 weapon (one is reminded of the story of the F-111 pilot who, newly arrived in southeast Asia, was asked "Do you have smart missiles?" and replied, "No, we have smart airplanes"). The one recent exception is the GBU-15, Rockwell's modular guided weapon system, which fits precision guidance to either a 2,000lb bomb or to the CBU-75 clustered munition dispenser. This has been certified for use from all TAC F-111 models, which can carry one on each of the four pylons. This TV/data-link system is normally part of the major F-111 force update which also includes the installation of the Pave Tack system in the weapons bay.

Deployment and Combat

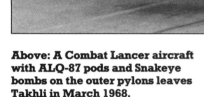

In March 1968, only eight months after TAC had received its first One-Eleven, six of the new bombers were deployed to Thailand for operations over North Vietnam. Within weeks half the force had been lost, but the lessons learned were put to good use when the type returned in 1972. Escalating costs and media criticism had taken their toll, however, and the current force is thinly spread, with most units having a mixture of variants, and maintenance problems further compounded by shortages of spares. Nevertheless, the F-111 remains one of NATO's most capable long-range penetration bombers.

By 1967 GD had flown all 18 RDT&E (research, development, test and evaluation) aircraft of the Air Force F-111A, as well as over 50 production aircraft. On the other hand Cat I (Category I, testing by the prime contractor, in this case GD) was nowhere near completed, and Cat II (by USAF Systems Command) had not even started. There was pressure on the Air Force not only to get the big new bird into the squadrons but to fly some effective missions to try to counter the torrent of highly adverse publicity in the media.

The first chance to gain favourable headlines came on May 22, 1967, when two production aircraft, still in contractor's hands, were flown across the North

Below: F-111As of the 474th TFW over the Pacific heading for Thailand on Combat Lancer deployment. A KC-135 provided tanker support.

Atlantic. One landed at RAF Wethersfield to give USAFE (USAF Europe) their first sight of what was slated to be one of their most potent weapons in the years to come. The other went on to Le Bourget for the Paris Air Show. Like its companion it had taken off from Loring AFB, Maine, and flown non-stop without air refuelling, completing the mission in 5 hours 54 minutes with 2½ hours fuel remaining. The pilot was Maj Tom Wheeler, and the unprecedented flight for a fighter-type aircraft at last drew grudging admission from the media that the F-111 might in fact be quite an airplane.

The urgent task of clearing the aircraft for service delivery was complicated by the fact that up to No 42 no two F-111As were exactly alike, though often the differences were small. Flying rates increased markedly in 1967, and by mid-year it was clear that the stipu-

lated 35 maintenance man-hours per flight hour would be likely to be met. At last, on July 17, Col Ivan H. Dethman, cigar-smoking CO of Detachment I, 448th TFS, collected the first of TAC's One-Elevens and flew it to Nellis AFB, north of Las Vegas.

Operational testing

Cat III (user unit) testing could thus begin, and though everyone had much to learn Dethman's style was to work men and aircraft around the clock, in a gruelling programme called Harvest Reaper. Officially the F-111A became operational with the 448th in October, in which month each aircraft on strength flew an average of 59·7 hours, which was actually fractionally lower than the figure for September but double the 30 hours demanded by the Air Force.

Few people liked the side-by-side cockpit, but on the whole initial impressions were highly favourable. Gradually the P-3 engine, attack and TF radars, ECM gear and other items became universal on all aircraft, and as crew skills increased so did confidence in flying lone missions deep into hostile territory. It took a while to trust one's life to the TFR, and it was found that heavy rain was interpreted as solid ground and, as it might start at a great height, some crews found themselves at plus-

Above: A Combat Lancer aircraft with ALQ-87 pods and Snakeye bombs on the outer pylons leaves Takhli in March 1968.

3g and at 10,000ft (3,000m) AGL before they could take over manually and dive back to what were supposed to be safer levels "in the weeds".

Another item that took some getting used to was the crew module. Everyone appreciated the comfort of not having to wear a parachute, but traditional ejection seats and parachutes were known quantities. A former GD flight test engineer, 'Ted' Tate, recalls: "For months Col Henry Brown, a 17-victory P-51 ace, had been giving me pure hell about the 'Chinese New Year, Mickey Mouse' escape system, which he was sure would fail to work at the vital moment. He was airborne with Maj Joe Jordan (F-104 altitude record-holder) on gun tests, when gun gas in the weapon bay exploded, causing mortal damage. These gentlemen had a very smooth ride back to Earth. Col Brown's Command magazine wanted him to write about it, and his article was filled with superlatives of praise for the system he had condemned the previous day".

Everyone wanted to prove the One-Eleven a winner, and air shows were attended whenever possible. On

Armed Forces Day Fred Voorhies, GD test pilot, put on a sparkling show at Holloman AFB, and then came in at minimum speed in dirty configuration with everything hanging out and down. He planned to clean up, hit afterburner, sweep the wings and go into a steep climb. To his horror he found he had got into the 'back of the drag curve' in which, as speed falls further, drag actually increases. He slammed the throttles wide open but could not avoid hitting the ground violently just short of the runway. When the dust cleared Fred could be seen climbing out. He took off his helmet and drop-kicked it (football style) far into the desert; then he pounded the One-Eleven with his fists, yelling "Dumbhead . . . Dumbhead . . ." All this in front of major network TV cameras. Later the extremely capable Voorhies flew the One-Eleven spin programme.

Deployment to Vietnam

By the start of 1968 TAC had demonstrated takeoffs and landings at light weights with ground rolls less than 2,000ft (600m), carried bombloads up to 29,000lb (13 tonnes), made 40 refuelling hook-ups in a single flight, and achieved navigational accuracies described as "eight times better than TAC's next-best fighter/bomber" and bombing accuracies that were "consistently amazing". The Joint Chiefs of Staff took a political decision to take a calculated risk and send six aircraft from the Nellis 428th TFS to Vietnam in the expectancy that they would prove the concept of deep interdiction by individual unescorted aircraft, with no backup from tankers, ECM or any other aircraft, and show what the One-Eleven could do. The project was called Combat Lancer, and the Detachment was put in Col Dethman's charge, as CO of the squadron.

They crossed the Pacific in a group, accompanied by a single KC-135 simply to take care of any fuel emergency, without even carrying drop tanks and navigating on the F-111 inertial systems. Litton could take pride in hitting the tiny island of Guam right on the nose after an uncorrected flight of 3,000 miles (4,800km) from Hickam AFB, Hawaii. The force arrived at Takhli Royal Thai AFB, 85 miles north of Bangkok on March 17, 1968. They flew a few training sorties in the unfamiliar environment and then began the arduous task of

flying long missions by night, completely alone, no matter what the weather. Typically they carried 24 Mk 82 bombs and two ALQ-87 pods.

The result was quite unexpected. On March 28 a One-Eleven went out on a mission and never came back. The same thing happened two days later, and again on April 27. As each crew planned its own mission and thereafter maintained radio silence, nobody had the slightest idea what had happened. Altogether 55 missions were flown in Combat Lancer, most by night and more than half in bad weather. Yet the 52 missions that came back reported complete success: they achieved what appeared to be total surprise, and the

Above: A classic photograph of TFR operations over Vietnam in 1968, showing an F-111A with wings at intermediate setting 'skiing' up a peak.

RHAWS and ECM receivers did not once indicate any illumination by a hostile radar, nor was there the slightest evidence of combat damage. Yet half the force had simply vanished. This was not at all what the Air Force had wanted, or expected; predictably, the media took it for granted the missing aircraft had been shot down.

Fortunately one of the crews had managed to eject. Their testimony, and examination of the crashed aircraft, made it clear there had been a sudden

catastrophic failure in the tailplane system, and this was traced to fatigue failure of a welded joint in the power unit of the left tailplane. Its effect would be to put the aircraft into a violent left roll and pitch-up, whilst slamming the sticks back into the crew's stomachs. On May 8, before the cause had been pinpointed, a Nellis aircraft was lost in precisely these circumstances. This accident was positively attributed to failure of the weld. Loss of six aircraft (three in Vietnam) in just over 5,000

Below: F-111As were used in the Igloo White programme to drop sensors which picked up sounds or vibrations from Viet Cong trucks.

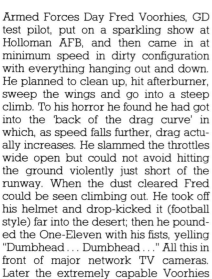

Left: A Combat Lancer aircraft landing after an air test at Takhli, without MERs on the pylons. Note the Combat Lancer badge on the rudder.

Top: A fine picture taken during the early years of training missions from Nellis AFB, Nevada. The aircraft is the 105th F-111A (including RDT&E).

Above: Similar externally, apart from the Triple Plow 2 inlets, this F-111F (then with the 389th TFS, 366th TFW) is a totally different weapon system.

hours flying with the Air Force was a record that compared very well with other supersonic types, but it is galling to think that, had the weld failures been avoided by different design or stricter quality-control the total would probably have been just one aircraft.

This was only the start of a prolonged period of major structural problems which were totally unexpected and which should have been avoided by the extremely comprehensive test programme carried out by GD and its suppliers. The structural heart of the aircraft is the WCTB (wing carry-through box) which carries the 8½in (21·6cm) pins on which the wings pivot. Ruling material of this massive component is Ladish D6AC, a high-strength steel known for its good ductility and freedom from brittle fracture which earned particularly good marks during the TFX bid evaluations. The precision-

fit bolts holding the WCTB together were carefully mated with holes reamed and ground to avoid the slightest scratch or sharp edge, yet in static fatigue testing potentially catastrophic cracks were discovered in late 1968 around several bolt-holes. An order went out restricting all F-111s to +3·5g manoeuvres until GD had taken each aircraft back and added 500lb (227kg) of thick reinforcing gussets. This cost several million dollars. Then on December 22, 1969, the left wing came clean off a Nellis aircraft being flown quite properly and with a fully reinforced WCTB. The crew did not have time to trigger the capsule.

All aircraft grounded

This was perhaps the all-time low point in the entire F-111 programme. The 223 aircraft then flying were grounded while the holiday period was spent in a frantic investigation to discover if any further flaws lurked in the WCTB or wing pivots. One F-111A was found to have a major flaw resembling a miniature bomb crater, about an inch across and extending almost the full depth of the D6AC steel, in the lower plate of the wing pivot fitting, which is the very strong area of the swinging outer wing surrounding the pivot pin. How this

escaped three successive tests by ultrasonic and magnetic-particle means was a mystery, but the Scientific Advisory Board undertook the unprecedented step of ordering the inspection and proof testing of every single F-111 in existence. Four complete new test facilities had to be built, two at Fort Worth, one at Waco and one at Sacramento, in which the One-Elevens – some from as far afield as Upper Heyford, England – were bent and twisted to +7·33g and −2·4g with the wings at 56deg sweep after prior refrigeration to −40deg F (−40deg C). No flaw was found in a wing pivot, but two potential crashes may have happened on the ground when a tailplane pivot shaft broke at Forth Worth and a WCTB lower plate parted in tension at Sacramento. This test programme eventually embraced more than 330 aircraft of the USAF, including 70 of the new SAC bomber version, but not the 24 for the RAAF which were delayed for almost ten years.

The technical troubles which afflicted the One-Eleven in its early years were far outside anything normally encountered, and strongly suggested the malignant hand of fate. They certainly did not reflect any failure on the part of any contractor's design process or qual-

ity control, and in no way could be construed as evidence of what the notorious Senator William A. Proxmire called "an unsafe and defective plane". Today F-111s have flown more than a million hours, almost all in the most demanding conditions of high speed at low level and in every kind of weather. The fact that none of this ever gets into the newspapers is the best evidence of what kind of aircraft the F-111 really is.

The F-111 was never named, but by 1968 its universal 'pronunciation' of One-Eleven had been supplemented by an unofficial name as curious as it was inappropriate: Aardvark. Assuming that the reason had nothing to do with coming first in alphabetical listings, it stemmed purely from the aircraft's long nose, also a feature of the South African animal whose name literally means earth-pig. The name was *not* chosen because of the One-Eleven's ability to hug the ground!

The slightly modified F-111E, whose only real difference lies in improved inlets but not the improved engines, entered service at Cannon AFB in October 1969. Congress criticized GD for making so many of the A-model, with supposedly inadequate inlets, but the only real criticism is that there was inadequate money to buy uprated en-

Above: An unusual near-vertical view of two F-111As of the 430th TFS, 474th TFW, operating out of Nellis over the dry watercourses of Nevada.

Left: Another view of one of the same aircraft. Note the unpainted HF shunt aerial (diagonal stripe along the fin) and the white colour of the flexible strips which admit the rear of the swing-wing root.

Below: An F-111F flying in TF mode over Idaho mountains in 1972.

gines to make the F-111E's inlets have some value. To the men in the cockpit it is virtually impossible to tell from the aircraft's performance or handling whether they are in an A or an E, though the E was the first to introduce improved ECM, a slightly different TFR, automatic ballistics computing and the strike camera under the nose.

Though large numbers of One-Elevens had been delivered by 1972, the only combat-ready ones were still those of the 474th TFW at Nellis, and when it was decided to take the bull by the horns and send the F-111 back to Vietnam the choice fell not on the 428th, the Combat Lancer veterans, but on the wing's other two squadrons, the 429th and 430th. The Viet Cong forces from the North had broken through into the South in April 1972 and not only was help wanted but it looked like being an opportunity really to put the One-Eleven to work in a way that might never return. This time the F-111A was a mature weapon system and the involvement was on a major scale, with two squadrons each of 24 aircraft, and they stayed for five months. It was called Constant Guard Five.

The two squadrons were determined to do it right, and if possible not only demonstrate what a fine interdiction platform can do but also set new records of many kinds. They planned to start by arriving at Takhli and straightaway flying a combat mission. To make this a sensible objective the 429th sent

Top: Two of the first F-111As to join the Air Force flying with a full load of 'slicks' with the 428th TFS, 474th TFW, from Nellis AFB in 1967.

Above: Another aircraft of the 474th, in this case with the wings at the intermediate position. Unusually, no badges are carried by this F-111A.

six crews on ahead to get some rest and plan their mission, while other crews ferried the aircraft, departing Nellis on September 27. They went 13½ hours non-stop to Andersen (Guam) with four tanker hook-ups. The last 6½ hours needed a single tanker hook-up over the Philippines, and a final run at high speed and low level across South Vietnam to check out all the systems. Everything was fine, the aircraft arrived fully serviceable and the combat crews were waiting.

About four hours were available for servicing, then after nightfall the mission – to RP-5 (Route Package 5) in northwest Vietnam – was on. Three of the six aircraft aborted with equipment failure prior to takeoff, the fourth had ECM failure in the air and aborted, another could not hit the primary target and had to choose the alternate, and the last never came back. Such was the unimpressive start to what was to become the opening of a new chapter in air warfare. The One-Eleven had been planned as the first of the new generation of sophisticated attack aircraft able to make deep interdiction penetrations of heavily defended regions and bomb with great precision and with no external assistance whatsoever.

In fact, so lone a game did the One-Elevens play that when aircraft did go missing nobody had the slightest idea whereabouts they might have gone in. The crews were more than happy to accept the serious consequences of not being found by their friends in return for guaranteed security of the mission. Security in South Vietnam had the reputation of being the leakiest of sieves, and if a crew did its own planning, worked out its own routes, profiles, turn points, radar offsets and target run-up, there was a fair chance that this information would not be passed to the enemy. But it was not long before four aircraft had been lost – all with a callsign ending in 3 and all on a Monday night – and political pressure came even from Washington itself for all crews to file detailed flight plans, and to call the airborne command post by radio at each turn point. This was most unpopular. Flight plans as filed were fragmentary, and at 450 knots at 300ft in foul weather on a pitch-black night the pilot and WSO had plenty to do without chatting with people interested in one's precise whereabouts and timing for the next turn point.

By late 1972 the defences were tremendous. In the Hanoi/Haiphong area flak was denser than over wartime targets in the Ruhr, and SAM sites were numbered in scores. The One-Elevens were facing this very much 'for real', and their crews were often frankly at the very limit of what their nerves could stand in demonstrating to the world that they could hack the new kind of air warfare. The idea of getting 'under the radar' was a joke: early warning, AAA and SAM radars were on every mountain, hill and small eminence, and it was not uncommon for the RHAWS lights to be on for minutes at a time, with occasional bursts of warning from the IRWS as well, watching from the top of the fin.

Never before had lone crews each of two men personally planned their mission and pitted their skill and courage against perhaps 20,000 people determined to stop them. How random could the route be? What about double-bluff, and repeating the previous route exactly (something ordinarily never done)? Dare one go through the middle of this narrow defile, or through that narrow gorge? What height AGL would be best at each point? Would a Hard Ride be possible? The vicious faces of the outcrops of karst, a kind of blackish limestone, meant that selecting Hard would almost pull the wings off, first going up to breast the crest and then bending the wings down to seek the bottom of the terrain on the far side. This was worse than any terrain in Nevada, and crews found it "absolutely incapacitating". Medium Ride was preferred except in fairly open country.

Pilots' impressions

Several crews talked about their low-level 'skiing' missions to *Air Force Magazine*. Former F-105 jock Capt Jackie Crouch said: "Think about flying around in daylight and good weather only 200ft above the ground, and going up and down over hills and into valleys, keeping this height. Now do this at night, in mountains and in heavy cloud when you can't see anything outside the cockpit. This is really, really exciting, even without the enemy threat.

"It takes real discipline to come up over these mountains, as we did at

Right: An F-111D of the 27th TFW, Cannon AFB, New Mexico, USAF 68-151. It is fitted with the internal gun and two practice bomb dispensers.

Below: Today F-111s have low-visibility markings, with tail code, insignia (except for unit badges) and stencils in black.

night, out on top of the cloud layer in the moonlight. We'd see those jagged peaks all round us poking through the cloud tops, and we'd have to put the nose down back into that mist. And as we went down the moonlight would fade, and the cloud get darker, and we'd know we were descending far below those peaks and were depending on our radars and our autopilots – and with Hanoi coming up. I won't say that I wasn't worried.

"One night, when the weather was *very* bad, I was in cloud for the last 11 minutes before bombs away. That means at the lowest level of the whole flight, at 250 or 200ft going up and down the hills. We didn't see a thing outside the cockpit, not even after the bombs left us. For me, this thing was really remarkable. Even now I can't explain how fantastic it was ... the confidence I gained in the airplane, it made a believer out of me. Given a choice on a

night strike of going in Hi or going in Lo, I'll take Lo, every time. And I'll go anywhere in the F-111."

To give the WSO's viewpoint Lt Steve Glass recalled the mission he flew on December 18, 1972 at the start of a critical Linebacker II period that took on the massed SAMs that were knocking down the B-52s, and effectively silenced them. "The delta weather was way down, ceiling 200ft or thereabouts and cloud piled up to 28,000ft.... We came skiing down the mountains and plunged out into the open under the lower edge of the overcast, and it seemed to us the entire Hanoi Valley was lit up like Las Vegas. Hanoi was bright with neon and street lights and the port of Haiphong was aglow in the distance. On the roads leading out of town and on the mountain switchbacks to the south the truck headlights were blazing like strings of pearls.

"We happened to arrive about ten minutes to eight in the evening, Hanoi time. We were coming so fast we were almost on release point before any of those lights started going out. Sections of the town blacked out one at a time, and we knew sirens were screaming and somebody down there was pulling master switches, even as the bombs left us."

The 429th and 430th flew over 4,000 missions, more than 3,980 of them in the TF mode at low level, and took just six losses, the lowest of any attack aircraft in actual warfare. This is despite the intense defences, the very limited number of targets and the extreme alertness, skill and long practice of the enemy gunners, radar operators and SAM crews. So far as is known, every one of the 74,000 bombs dropped by the F-111s was on target; in the case of one vital target, surrounded by Hanoi city, which was 'off limits', no other type of aircraft was permitted to bomb it, but the F-111s made repeated attacks, all at very high speed at low level and in all weathers, and destroyed it without one bomb falling outside the small target area. The two squadrons rotated back to Nellis from January 1973, the last mission being the 4,030th on February 22.

Deployment to England

No other version of F-111 except the A has actually gone to war. The next model in service, the E, was transferred from Cannon AFB to re-equip the 20th TFW which was re-formed at RAF Upper Heyford, Oxfordshire. The first pair of Es swept in from a leaden sky on September 12, 1970 and found that the old RAF base was being torn apart for new facilities including simulators, full-size training rigs (for example, for the fuel and wing-sweep systems) and an awesome amount of maintenance capability.

The three squadrons, the 55th, 77th and 79th, at first each had their own tail codes, and altogether the base built up to an active establishment, excluding dependents, of about 4,000, many of whom are at two satellite fields, Barford St John and Croughton. Though aircraft of the 20th have to keep in practice at tanker hook-ups they need no such support in Europe, nor any forward operating base. From the heart of England they can fly every mission with which they are tasked by the NATO commanders, and their low-level training missions frequently pass within a few feet of shepherds high in the Alps as they thunder in TF flight to drop practice bombs on the range at Aviano in the foothills above Venice. Early in the F-111 era no aircrew were posted to fly the type unless they had at least 1,000 hours, including 750 hours jet time. Conversion has always taken place at Nellis, typically with 13 missions in 45 hours' flying, followed by a further 13 trips upon joining the user squadron.

The totally different F-111D began at last to come off the production line at aircraft No 216 in autumn 1970. Service entry took place from October 1971 with the only unit ever to operate this model, the 27th TFW at Cannon AFB, New Mexico, replacing the wing's F-111As. Deliveries were completed in February 1973, and the 27th have ever since maintained an image which bravely accentuates the fact that F stands for Fighter. The gun is normally carried, together with the occasional AIM-9 Sidewinder, and though the 27th do not reckon to be second-best to anyone in air/ground delivery, they have been successful in projecting their belief that they fly the best One-Elevens ever built. It is significant that in 1979, when the USAF was urgently trying to get Congress to agree on a stretching programme to turn TAC and SAC F-111s into long-range FB-111B/Cs, as described in a later chapter, they picked the F-111Ds of the 27th as those best suited to conversion. A cynic would say it is because they are already so non-standard, and hard and expensive to maintain.

Last of the tactical attack versions, and last new-built One-Eleven of any sort, the F-111F seeks to get the best avionics features of the D but at less cost, plus the increased flight performance from the excellent P-100 engine. In fact this engine was not ready when the F-111F replaced the D at the 456th aircraft, and the first 30 were delivered with the same P-9 engine as the D. The Mk IIB avionics likewise were not fully available, and it took about a further year for the USAF to receive a fully developed F-111F. This is certainly the best all-round F-111, not so much because of the engine but because it offers considerably greater mission/avionic capabilities than the A and E (virtually identical to those of the D) with considerably fewer and less-costly problems and with a higher availability and reliability. The engine certainly confers improved performance, which every F-111 crew would appreciate, but this is very seldom of any significance because it is possible to fly the missions on

Left: An early picture of the eighth F-111E before application of unit insignia. Note the clearly visible ECM flush aerials on the nose.

Above: View from a KC-135 boomer's station of two F-111E aircraft of the 20th TFW, Upper Heyford, refuelling over solid cloud in 1980.

Below: When the 20th TFW was first re-equipped with the F-111E the tail codes differed for each squadron. JT was the 77th TFS.

the old low-powered P-3 engine. Indeed, though the P-100 is in every way a much better engine than any previous TF30, its extremely high price was the chief reason for the small number of F-models built. Buying them in a small trickle, 12 a year in the final four years, also helped to make the price soar, and it is small wonder that the 12 for 1975 were cancelled.

Idaho to Thailand

The F joined the 347th TFW at Mountain Home AFB, Idaho, in February 1972, where there is plenty of rugged country and extremes of weather. The aircraft were only with the 347th little over a year; in 1973 the wing was ordered to Thailand, flying F-111As, and the very last combat mission in the SEA (southeast Asia) theatre was flown by one of the 347th's swing-wingers over Cambodia on August 15, 1973, closing out nine years of non-stop warfare.

The F-111Fs were reassigned to the 366th TFW, still at Mountain Home and with unchanged MO tail codes, even when in August 1976 one squadron, called 366 Detachment 1, was temporarily sent to the Republic of Korea to show that sudden belligerence by North Korea had not gone unnoticed. The Fs did particularly well to make the totally overwater transit to Taegu AB in just 11½ hours elapsed time from Idaho. On return from Korea the 366th had only another few months before, like the 347th, they had to switch to the Brand-X

Above: The first mission from RAF Lakenheath by the 48th TFW, on April 9, 1977. Note the white tail codes and the blister for the gun.

Left: The 48th Wing Commander's F-111F photographed in June 1981 during the RAF Strike Command Tac Bombing Competition. By this time the tail codes were in black.

Right: An F-111E, 68-062, being delivered by the 20th TFW to British Aerospace at Filton for major rework and refurbishing in April 1982.

Below: Air-to-air of F-111F 70-2369 of the 48th TFW, still with white tail codes in late 1978.

Above: A 1983 portrait of one of the 48th TFW's F-111Fs showing the large bulge of the Pave Tack (also visible in the photograph at centre left). Under the wings are four Paveway II (GBU-16B/B of 1,000lb size) laser-guided 'smart bombs'.

version, the F-111A. Their aircraft were taken from them and ferried non-stop on internal fuel to RAF Lakenheath, Suffolk, where they replaced the F-4D Phantoms of the 48th TFW in March 1977.

After conversion the 48th worked up quickly to combat-ready status, unquestionably becoming the most formidable long-range interdiction outfit in the entire European theatre (on the NATO side, at least). Despite weather markedly more depressing than Idaho, the Fs

settled down to hard work of many kinds, some of it classified, and put up an enviable safety record which in 1982–83 was suddenly shattered by the loss of six aircraft in as many months, two of the crews failing to eject and one aircraft, in May 1983, simply going straight into the North Sea on return from a mission, with no radio call. The importance of the 48th is shown by its selection as one of the first USAF units to be completely equipped with Pave Tack, as described earlier. The next chapter tells more.

Servicing in England

Location of what are for geographical reasons the two most important F-111 wings in the United Kingdom clearly means that, over a long period, aircraft

have to be maintained more than 5,000 miles (8000km) away from the true parent organization, the Air Force Logistics Command's Sacramento Air Logistics Center at McClellan AFB. For almost a decade the USAF either ferried or shipped One-Elevens all the way to California for major overhaul. Then in 1978 it put out an exploratory contract with British Aerospace. The Weybridge-Bristol Division was given a small package of maintenance work on UK-based F-111s including renewal of the pyrotechnics of the cockpit ejection capsule. This is a particularly tricky and crucial task, which has to be repeated every four years; moreover, though the crews' lives depend on it, it can hardly be functionally tested after renewal!

Bristol did so well on this first contract

that by 1983 work had built up to a complete major overhaul of 20 F-111 aircraft a year, from both Upper Heyford (Es) and Lakenheath (in mid-1983 temporarily detached to Sculthorpe while Lakenheath runways are resurfaced) which has the F model. Aircraft are completely torn apart, and continued excellent performance was rewarded in 1983 by the offer of a four-year contract instead of an annual one, with throughput raised to between 36 and 40 aircraft per year. The work is done in the former 'Brabazon Hangar' where Concordes were later assembled. Since 1982 aircraft have been given low-voltage formation light strips and a complete repainting to the new strict specification before being returned to their units.

Flying the Mission

The author was once privileged to fly a training mission in a One-Eleven, but that single flight, memorable though it was, hardly qualifies him to write about flying it, or even in it. We asked a member of the 493rd Tactical Fighter Squadron, 48th Tactical Fighter Wing, United States Air Force, to tell us in simple terms what it is like. Captain Jim Rotramel is widely known to aviation readers, and especially to plastic modellers, but in between the demands of a heavy and very varied workload he finds time to climb into the right seat of an F-111F.

What's it like to fly the F-111?

That's a question that Aardvark drivers – like all fighter pilots – get asked a lot. It would seem to be an easy question to answer, but it's not. I've read many "pilot reports", but quoting a mountain of statistics has never imparted what it FEELS like to fly a fast jet – and the F-111 is one of the fastest. So this pilot's report, written by a weapon systems operator, is going to be different.

Perhaps we should start with who flies F-111s. There are two of us, sitting side-by-side: the pilot – we call him the AC, for aircraft commander – on the left and the navigator/weapons systems operator – known professionally as WSO, pronounced "wizzo" – on the right, both officers.

Pilots have gone through a year of undergraduate pilot training, and WSOs through at least six months of undergraduate navigator training. After completing these schools they go to lead-in fighter training for a couple of months, to learn the basics of flying fighters in aircraft that are familiar to the pilots, allowing them to concentrate on the flying instead of the airplane.

Only then do they begin flying the Aardvark – the F-111's unofficial, but universally accepted, nickname. It takes about a year for a newcomer to the airplane to become MR, mission ready. It takes almost another year to become comfortable with operating all of the systems in this very complex war machine.

Our missions begin with flight planning. They're planned to help us accomplish a set of tasks we're required to perform every six months. An individual mission takes anywhere from a couple of hours to a couple of days to plan. The actual day of the flight, the crew shows up to take care of the final details about 3½ hours before takeoff, and conduct a briefing an hour later.

About an hour before takeoff time we "step" to whichever aircraft the maintenance section has assigned us that day. Although AC and WSO names are stencilled on the nosegear doors, it's only by chance if we actually fly "our own" jet.

The jet is BIG. Our internal fuel load weighs more than a fully loaded F-16! Technically a fighter by designation, it's really a tactical bomber, roughly combining the range and payload of a B-66 with the speed and manoeuvrability of an F-105.

The AC does the detailed walk-around inspection, while the WSO checks any external stores and does a quick look at the jet before climbing on board and strapping in. The cockpit, by fighter standards, is quite roomy – simi-lar to the front of a compact-sized (ie, European) car. The seats are very hard – especially after we have been strapped into one for more than three hours! But that hardness helps protect us from serious injuries if we have to eject. Unlike all other fighters, the F-111 doesn't have ejection seats, but an escape capsule. In an ejection, the entire cockpit area separates from the airplane. This virtually eliminates the wind-blast injuries which can be encountered when ejecting at high airspeeds in other aircraft. More than one F-111 crew owe their lives to this feature.

Ready for takeoff

Engine start comes 45 minutes prior to takeoff, and for the next 25 minutes we're busy powering up and checking out all the different systems. Twenty minutes before takeoff, we taxi to the runway where we're checked over one last time. Once on the runway and cleared for takeoff, the engines are run up – first to military (MIL) power and then into the afterburner range, one at a time, while we check them out.

At brake release, power to both engines is increased to maximum afterburner, and we accelerate quickly but smoothly to 145 knots, when the AC rotates the nose up, followed shortly by liftoff. The takeoff roll takes 15 seconds and 2,500 feet for an F model, which, with engines even more powerful than the F-15's, is noticeably quicker than other F-111s.

A typical training sortie will include an hour of high-level cruise, a half-hour of low-level practice, with 15 minutes or more dropping practice bombs. If we've enough fuel left, we will practise various types of landing approaches when we get home.

After a 2½ to 3-hour flight, it will take another hour to park the jet, debrief any maintenance problems, and get back to the squadron for a flight debriefing and paperwork session (even this job isn't done until the paperwork is finished!) taking about another hour. As you can see, flying just once is an all-day affair.

A lasting impression is the amount of

Above: About to start engines of an F-111F of the 390th TFS (Detachment 1 of the 366th TFW) prior to the first mission from Taegu in August 1976.

Right: A departure sequence from the Forth Worth runway of 74-0188, the 106th F-111F and 562nd and last One-Eleven. It was accompanied by an even more sprightly performer, the first YF-16A – which, unlike the One-Eleven, is in MIL (dry) power.

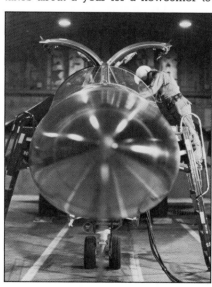

Above: A pilot of the 48th TFW runs through his checks prior to entering the cockpit of his F-111F inside its HAS (hardened aircraft shelter) at RAF Lakenheath in 1983.

Right: A different photographer took this picture a few minutes later as the aircraft exited the HAS.

Above: A March 1983 photograph of an aircraft of the 48th TFW, 70-2399, carrying practice-bomb dispensers and an ALQ-131 jammer pod.

flame which comes out the engines in full afterburner. The only thing I've seen that belches more fire is the SR-71. One young observer of an F-111 takeoff at night said it appeared they were "riding on a star". I can't think of a more apt description.

With all the flame comes a lot of noise. Which is probably why F-111 bases are usually situated far from large popula-tion centres. All that is more noticeable when watching an F-111 than when flying one. In the Aardvark it's imposs-ible to see your own engine, tail, or inner portions of the wings. The ear-splitting blast of the engines is virtually unnoticeable in the cockpit, where the noise level is comparable to a commer-cial airliner.

Despite its ungainly appearance on the ground, when the gear comes up and the wings go back, the true purpose of the airplane's design becomes clear – SPEED. Ask any air-to-air fighter pilot how much fun it is to convert on an F-111 flying at 200 feet doing 570 knots or more. The little folded wing, that makes us one of the slowest-turning airplanes around, also lets us go as fast and low as we can stand – and with a ride that's normally as smooth as glass.

The wings are swept with a small handle on the left wall, mounted above the pilot's throttles. There's a gauge we can both see to tell us what angle they're at, and they're manually swept to provide the best flying qualities for any given aircraft weight and speed. From the right seat, you notice a faint jerk when the wings begin moving, but

Below: Pulling negative g down the slope to TFR height over Loch Ness, Scotland, on a practice mission by the 48th in June 1982.

Below: Another view from the right-hand seat of an F-111F, in this case of mountainous terrain passing the wingtip at 450 knots.

Foot of page: The low-voltage strip lights stand out on this F-111F of 494 TFS, 48 TFW (70-2384) snapped from its companion in May 1983.

Above: Taken in December 1982, a fine air-to-air of 70-2366 over rugged terrain. Terrain-following flight would be much lower.

aside from that it doesn't feel any different than any other airplane.

We earn our keep by carrying substantial payloads at high-subsonic cruise speeds, at low altitudes, and in any weather, deeper into enemy territory than other non-strategic aircraft could even imagine. Cruising at eight miles a minute, 500 feet off the ground, is exciting and beautiful. You're low enough to get a really good look at the countryside, and in the United Kingdom that's rugged coastlines, lakes, mountains and castles. After a while, 500 feet seems quite high – you can get comfortable there, at least in daylight.

On the other hand, 200 feet never seems high – it's an incredible thrill, but one you never take for granted, especially when approaching the speed of sound. The sensation of speed is amazing, and if the pilot decides to convert all that airspeed into altitude, your altimeter can read 15,000 feet in about 20 seconds! There's not a ride in a carnival anywhere that comes close to it.

Terrain Following, or "TFing", is what set the F-111 in a class by itself for more than a decade. The ability to fly as low as 200 feet AGL (above ground level) at

as fast as 1·2 times the speed of sound in almost any weather is of great tactical significance – not to mention scary! Flying at 1,000 feet AGL in mountainous terrain at night, while seeing nothing but the hazy grey/black of the inside of a cloud, punctuated only by the occasional red flash of the rotating beacon, is guaranteed to focus your attention on the task at hand, which is ensuring that the automatic TF system is working properly.

Terrain-following flight
Basically, what happens is that the TF antenna nods up and down, scanning a narrow sector in the aircraft's flight path to determine terrain elevation. This information is processed and transmitted to the flight control system which adjusts the aircraft's pitch attitude to avoid the ground. It's up to the pilot to make any necessary power adjustments. The actual path across the ground is determined by the points set into the navigational computers. Even though the aircraft has the ability to avoid the terrain in its path, it's up to the crew to plan a flight path which best uses the terrain to mask the airplane from enemy defences.

During TF flight, the atmosphere on board becomes very businesslike, the small talk ceases, and we each monitor our instruments to make sure everything is working as intended. The com-

mentary is terse; we each tell the other only what we see in front of us. The AC monitors the aircraft response to the terrain depicted on his TF radar presentation. This, combined with the larger picture of the terrain that the WSO is describing to him from his attack-radar presentation, indicates a properly functioning system. Safe TFing requires excellent crew coordination, which means practice and trust. Complacency towards TFing is unwise and could be fatal. We may argue about the percentage lethality of Triple-A or SAMs, but we all know the ground rates 100 per cent.

Questions about performance are difficult to answer. For instance, "How fast do you go?" Normally, we roar by at about 480 knots, but if someone is trying to shoot us down, we go as fast as we can stand it. It also depends on the speed limits of the bombs we're carrying or their fuzes, as well as a lot of other things. The airplane itself certainly isn't speed-limited!

Maximum speeds
There's no quoted top speed for the F-111. When the skin temperature gets hot a timer begins counting the number of seconds it can keep up the speed before parts start to weaken from the heat. In reality, that type of speed performance is of little practical value, since, while it's possible to outrun an

attacker, it would also quickly exhaust our fuel. A kill is a kill, be it by gun, missile or a case of the terminal stupids!

The same answer applies to "How far can you go?" and "How much can you carry?" All those classic yardsticks of performance really don't work well in the real world. There are too many shades of grey for a simple black-and-white answer.

What you can count on is that our mission in a real war would be tailored to get us to our target and back with as many of the right type of bombs as we could carry. The further away the target, the fewer the number of bombs. At any rate, we wouldn't expect to come home with loads of gas sloshing around our fuel tanks!

This small piece of the F-111 story wouldn't be complete without a few words about the people on the ground. They're legion, from the mail clerks and cooks, to the security police and families. Their work, support and tolerance makes our job possible. But most of all, the maintenance people: for even though the Aardvark is a magnificent and capable airplane, it's not as maintainable as the new airplanes which have benefited from its experience. So that we can do our job, a lot of young people have to work long hours, sometimes in miserable weather. Although the fliers get the glory, we never forget whose shoulders we stand on.

The Bombers

Nobody can turn a fighter into a strategic bomber, but when the fighter is the One-Eleven there is enough internal fuel to make the idea worth careful study. For more than 20 years General Dynamics and the US Air Force have been only too keenly aware of the highly effective bombers that could be produced from today's F-111 by drastic modification, but Congress has never voted the money. Instead SAC has a small and elite force which flies a bomber only slightly different from the tactical models. Their consistently high scores in competition have been a source of embarrassment to the long-established SAC wings.

Since the earliest days of the TFX programme, SAC (USAF Strategic Air Command) had eyed the aircraft as a possible basis for a small supersonic bomber. The command never thought of just buying the resulting F-111, but the impressive range figures appeared to indicate the possibility of future stretching into a larger bomber to fly SAC missions. GD began work on possible SAC versions in 1962, and several were three-engined, with the centre engine fed by an S-duct. Other models had larger and more powerful engines, most of which existed only on paper, and at all times the SAC One-Eleven was regarded as suitable for the nuclear role only, the payload being used for fuel rather than for massive loads of conventional bombs.

In any case, it was clear that not even a stretched F-111 could fly the global missions of SAC, even with flight refuelling. Like the B-47 and GD's own B-58 before it, the F-111 could at best be a limited aircraft relying heavily on inflight refuelling and on some missions either departing from a forward operating location in a friendly country or recovering to a friendly base outside the United States, and in general being assigned to targets on the periphery of possible enemies.

Having pointed out its deficiencies it is fair to claim that the F-111 offered many advantages. Compared with the B-52, the command's only global carrier vehicle, it had a very much smaller radar cross-section, and could carry at least as good a suite of EW/ECM systems for its own protection. It could be made hard against nuclear explosion effects, where the B-52 was soft. It could fly much faster, at much lower heights above the ground. Its 'penetrability' was assessed as several times better, especially against the most heavily defended targets. Not least, it could be built from the start with more modern avionics, and in particular with a more precise navigation system.

In the course of 1964, while SAC hardened in its belief that the F-111 should form the basis for an interim low-level penetrator, ideas of gross stretching began to fade, on grounds of timing, cost and the demonstrable fact that most of the stretched models were still range-limited. What was called the FB-111 (later FB-111A) was first drawn in that year, combining a wing almost identical to the long-span wing of the Navy F-111B with a regular F-111A fuselage and tail but with main landing gears having larger tyres and increased-capacity brakes, to which were soon added strengthened legs to handle increased gross weights. The heaviest loading envisaged was two of the new SRAMs (short-range attack missiles) in the weapon bay and eight 600US-gal drop tanks under the wings, a configuration never realized in practice. Flight crew were to number three, comprising pilot, copilot/navigator and defence-systems operator.

Thrust and weight

It was an important part of the concept of the FB that it need not have a thrust/weight ratio as high as a fighter version. Thus a third TF30 engine was not needed, even though from the start the gross weights were planned to be in the region of 100,000lb (45,000kg), at a time when it was hoped the 'fighter' model would gross about 55,000lb (25,000kg). What was completely unpredicted was that the so-called fighter models would themselves escalate in weight to the 100,000lb level, resulting in essentially the same thrust/weight ratio as for the SAC aircraft. Moreover, the TAC versions do not have the long-span wing.

Development of the FB was interwoven with models for two export customers, who were confidently expected to be the first of many. Back in 1963 Britain had hoped to sell its TSR.2 aircraft to Australia, but internal British troubles based on inter-service rivalry and narrow party politics had already begun to unite to torpedo this programme, and the Australians naturally began to doubt that TSR.2 could be relied upon. The obvious alternative was the F-111, and despite frantic pleas from the British, Aussie Prime Minister Menzies and Defence Minister Athol Townley signed on October 24, 1963 for 24 F-111s at a total 'ceiling price' of A$112 million, or US$90,749,040. It

Above: A 48th TFW One-Eleven is loaded with Snakeyes under pressure during the Quick Turnround section of the 1981 RAF Strike Command Bombing Competition.

Below: Inflight refuelling compatibility test with the eighteenth RDT&E F-111A, which served as the original FB prototype – complete with SAC badge.

seemed the obvious choice. Menzies said "No government could spend money on anything else", and to the charge that the price might escalate Townley replied "There is far more chance it will be reduced, because our figure is based on the present production run". This run was for 1,726 aircraft, more than three times the number actually built.

By 1965, when the FB was at the stage of detailed planning, the newly elected Labour government in Britain was determined to do away with TSR.2, and it cancelled the programme on April 6 of that year. In its election campaign that government had announced not only its intention to kill the homegrown aircraft but also its wish to replace it with the American TFX, which was presented to the British people as a far superior and much cheaper alternative. In the announcement of cancellation of TSR.2 the Ministry of Defence stated: "An order for 150 TSR.2 aircraft would have meant each one would have cost £5 million ... a full programme based on the F-111 would be £300 million less...." In other words, the RAF F-111s would cost £450 million in all, or £3 million each, "allowing for all future charges and payments". This was just double the price of the Australian aircraft, but still seemed much better than £5 million.

Britain and Australia engaged in detailed talks during 1965 both to sew up the contracts, which were not with GD but with the US Government, through the Department of Defense, and also to establish the precise standard of build of their respective aircraft. Both countries agreed to have the long-span wing, strengthened landing gear with larger tyres and brakes, and other features of

the SAC bomber version, which by the end of 1965 was designated FB-111A. The Australian (RAAF) aircraft became the F-111C and, though it was officially described as the F-111A by British spokesmen, the British (RAF) variant received the odd designation of F-111K. In February 1966 Defence Minister Healey announced that Britain was buying ten for a start, with a further 40 to follow in April 1967, at a 'ceiling price' of US$5·95 million each. This compared with a unit price of $7·8 million on the

original 1965 calculation (which saved £300 million) and $3·8 million for the Australians. There were to be 46 F-111Ks (XV902/947) and four TF trainers (XV884/887). The British involvement was convoluted in the extreme, and involved offset deals with the USA and third-party nations and much more besides, but fortunately the whole house of cards collapsed in January 1968 when Prime Minister Wilson announced that the F-111K had, like TSR.2, been cancelled.

Above: The seventh F-111A was used for stores separation tests with all eight pylons fitted. Such loads have never been carried, even by today's FB-111A.

By this time most of the parts had been made for all 50 aircraft, 19 were visible on the Fort Worth assembly line and the two YF-111K flight-test aircraft were almost complete and painted. Because of their close similarity to the FB-111A the decision was taken to convert

Right: An FB-111A over Lake Worth on contractor flight test. The configuration is that which would be used on most SAC missions in a nuclear war, with four tanks but no external weapons. The widely publicized bomb-toting capability of the FB is probably only of academic interest, though six tanks might be an important configuration giving intercontinental range.

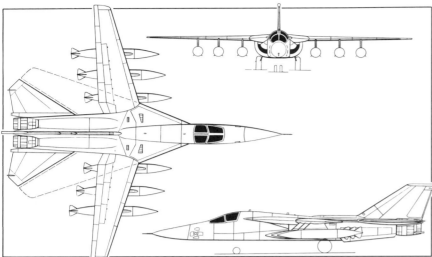

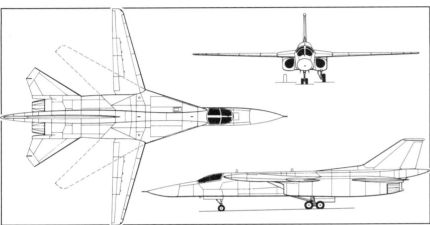

Above: Three-view of the FB-111A with six underwing tanks

Below: Three-view of the proposed FB-111H strategic bomber

as many F-111Ks as possible into this version, but the first two machines, both of them TFs, were too different for ready conversion. Eventually they were completed as YF-111A aircraft of the USAF (67-149/150) with provision for very complete instrumentation in R&D programmes, as explained in the last chapter. The other 48 were completed as FB-111As for SAC.

The force structure and detail design of the FB-111A were all settled during 1965, the only differences compared with the F-111E, with Triple-Plow II inlet, being the long-span wing, new main gears, Mk IIB avionics with an added astrocompass and other small variations, SRAM missile provisions, and the more powerful P-7 engine. This engine was the first uprated model to enter service, running well ahead of the less-powerful engine of the F-111D, and it stemmed from the Navy-sponsored P-12 engine of the defunct F-111B. In fact, the first two production FBs were delivered with P-12 engines, but were re-engined later with the standard P-7.

To speed development the 18th of the original development batch of F-111As, 63-9783, was completed as the FB-111A prototype. It flew in gull grey and white on July 30, 1967, and played the chief role in early proving of FB capabilities other than SRAM firing. The first production machine, 67-159, with tempor-

ary P-12 engines, flew on July 13, 1968 and handled the SRAM compatibility and launch programme during Cat II testing.

More than any other part of the F-111 programme the FB suffered from escalation in price. The stated intention had been to assign this new swing-wing bomber as a replacement for 345 B-52C, D and F heavy bombers and 80 B-58As and TB-58s. The planned force to do this numbered 210, plus 53 extra aircraft for use as spares and to make good attrition losses, and Defense Secretary McNamara said the total cost would be "in the order of a billion and three-quarters". Subsequently the specification for the FB-111A hardly altered beyond refinement of the avionic systems into the Mk IIB which also went into the F-111F with minor differences, but the general rise in price brought a reduction in the numbers bought to a mere 76, costing $1·2 billion, not far short of the total for 263.

First SAC unit
The first FB-111A unit was the 340th Bomb Group of SAC, which was specially formed to introduce the type to SAC service, while Systems Command was engaged in Cat II testing, and before Cat III tests of the complete FB-111A/SRAM system had started. The 340th received its first aircraft on September

25, 1969. Based at Carswell AFB, adjacent to the manufacturer's plant at Fort Worth, the 340th's principal role was to train FB-111A crews. Like all SAC units it set a very high standard in all things, the qualifications for pilots including more than 2,000 hours in command and at least two years in a combat-ready squadron, with at least 1,500 hours demanded of navigators.

The FB has dual flight controls, but the right-seater has an exceptional amount to do because EW/ECM is even more important in this model than in the tactical versions, and was at one time thought to merit the inclusion of a third crew-member. Initial crew training was handled by a unit of the 340th BG, the 4007th Combat Crew Training Squadron. Using selected material and with an outstanding navigation/bombing system in the FB-111A these small two-seaters quickly established a great reputation in SAC and fairly consistently have carried off top honours in the annual Bombing Competition. One of the crews from the 4007th took the chief awards at the 1970 competition, when the type was still

weeks away from becoming operational.

The first delivery to a user unit took place on December 16, 1970, when an FB was ferried by a crew of the 509th BW to their operating base at Pease AFB, New Hampshire. Ultimately SAC built up an active inventory of 70 aircraft, which has since been reduced to 58, assigned equally to the 509th, which handles crew training, and the rival 380th BW at Plattsburgh AFB, in upper New York, to which the 4007th was also relocated. Crews fly about four practice missions a month, each of 3½–4½ hours duration and involving hookups with a KC-135 (either of the USAF or, often, of a New England ANG unit) and plenty of low-level penetration including electronically scored free-fall bombing. Very occasionally a SRAM is fired, at White Sands Missile Range, New Mexico, but real SRAMs are seldom flown. SRAM accuracy has been consistently better than for the same missile fired from the B-52.

In general the emphasis in training is the maintenance of a very high degree of professional skill without burning

Right: In most respects the Royal Australian Air Force F-111C is similar to the FB-111A, though the avionics and engines are no more advanced than those of the original F-111A. Professional aircrew in 6 Sqn have become wholly attuned to a heavy but low-thrust aircraft which often has to fly in a tropical atmosphere.

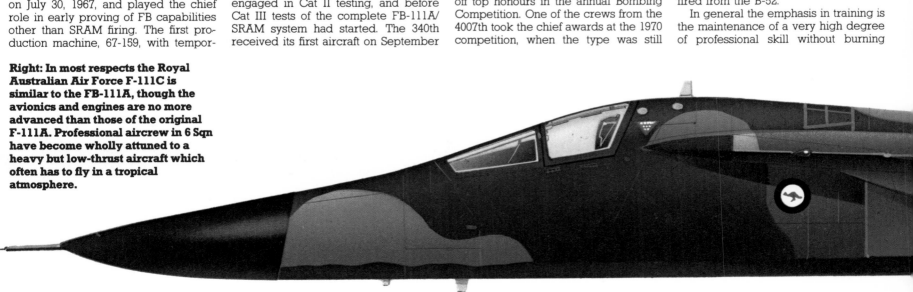

much fuel and without aircraft attrition (because FBs cannot be replaced). The much-publicized capability of flying with 50 Mk 117 bombs, each weighing a nominal 750lb (340kg) but in fact nearer to 825lb (374kg) and thus representing a total load of 41,250lb (18,711kg), is never even approached, and it is relatively unusual to fly with any significant load of conventional bombs. With the theoretical maximum load the ceiling is so poor that the aircraft could not clear the summit of Pike's Peak, Colorado, which is at 14,110ft (4,301m). The FB was castigated back in the 1960s on this account, but it is of no importance to an aircraft whose operational life is centred on altitudes below 1,000ft (300m) and often below 300ft (90m).

Today the normal maximum payload of the FB can be regarded as six free-fall nuclear bombs, such as the Mk 43 or Mk 57 or TX61, or six SRAMs, two internal and four on the four swivelling inner wing pylons. Quite often two bombs or SRAMS are carried internally and two or four tanks externally, but it is extremely rare for six pylons to be fitted, and there is no present plan ever

to fit the theoretical eight. Low-level bomb runs normally work up to Mach 0·75 or 495 knots (570mph/917km/h), and though it is common to practise stall recoveries there is no incentive to do anything that would eat into airframe fatigue life, because already the average fleet age of the FB is just over 13 years (October 1983) and they may well have to go on for a further 13.

Service experience has in general been exemplary. At the 100,000 hour mark, achieved in January 1976, there had been just two fatal accidents and a total of four write-offs. Performance in the SAC bombing and navigation competition has been consistently superior, largely because the FB has no other modern aircraft against which to compete – despite costly updating of the B-52G and H and the best efforts of their very experienced crews.

At the time of writing the most recent (November 1982) contest again proved a runaway win for the swing-wingers. The 509th BW took the Fairchild Trophy as the SAC wing with the highest bomber and tanker scores (the FB sharing the honours with the KC-135s of the

509th ARS). FB-111As have won this trophy in seven of the past eight years. The 509th also took the Mathis Trophy, awarded for maximum total points in both high and low-level bombing; FBs have taken this trophy in five of the previous six years. The 509th also took the John C. Meyer Trophy, awarded to the unit achieving the highest expectancy of damage on the basis of bombs delivered on target. The award for the best single FB-111A crew, however, was won by the rival 380th BW.

At the same meet the award for the Best F-111 Crew went to crew A-1 from the RAAF, who flew their F-111C all the way from Amberley, at Ipswich in southeast Queensland, 50 miles from Brisbane. The RAAF went into the One-Eleven programme with sky-high hopes

in 1963, and had not the slightest inkling that they would end up almost cancelling, and not receive a single aircraft Down Under for another ten years! Yet, despite the problems, the F-111C has given Australia interdiction muscle it has never had before, and will certainly never have again.

It will be recalled that the Australian government had signed for 24 aircraft in 1963 at a unit price of A$3·8 million, the build standard being essentially a mix of the F-111A airframe and engines with

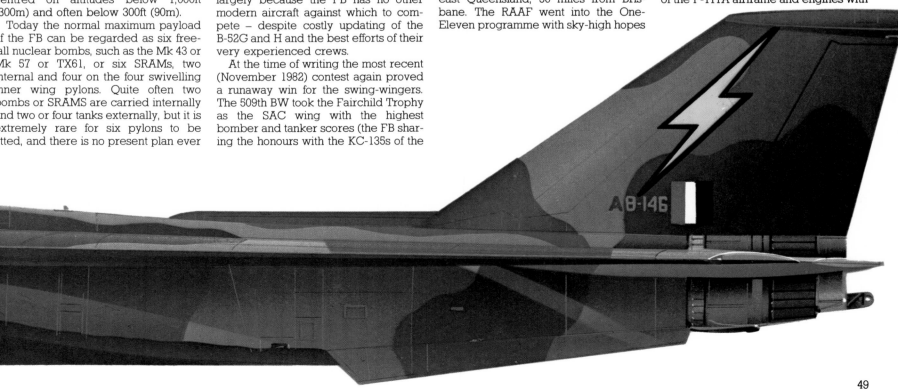

long-span wings and strengthened landing gear, and a removable stick on the right side, but retaining F-111A avionics. It was claimed the new wing and landing gear would 'significantly increase the range and payload', though as the fuel capacity is the same as for the F-111A the difference cannot be significant. In fact, the combination of a heavier aircraft with the least-powerful of all F-111 engines with early Triple Plow I inlets makes the F-111C theoretically the most sluggish model, with rate of roll reduced by the increased span, but the differences are unimportant because the aircraft can do all that has been asked of it. In theory it replaced the Canberra, but as the US supplied F-4E Phantoms as an interim stop-gap RAAF Nos 1 and 6 Sqns got a taste for air-combat capability which they were reluctant to part with.

Another complication was that in July 1966, by which time the manufacture of the RAAF aircraft had started, new Air Minister Peter Howson announced that

Below: The FB-111A aerodynamic prototype, originally the 18th RDT&E F-111A 63–9783, did a lot of flying with possible SAC loads, one of which was this combination of four tanks and two B61 nukes. In practice the external stores have invariably been tanks and SRAMs.

six aircraft would be flown back to the USA for conversion into RF-111Cs, with the USAF/GD removable multi-sensor pack in the weapon bay. Howson stressed "The striking power of the RAAF will not be affected, because the six modified aircraft can be reconverted to the strike role within hours". The Australian government made regular progress payments on its bill totalling A$7·98 million for RF-111C costs, but this project temporarily collapsed with termination of the RF-111A.

Delayed delivery

Training of F-111C maintenance crews began in 1967, with the start of flight-crew training following in 1968. It was admitted that delivery of the 24 aircraft would slip by about two months, being completed between September and December 1968, but structural problems caused further delays and a team led by Air Vice-Marshal E. Hey spent three weeks at Washington, Fort Worth and Nellis. Howson's successor, Gordon Freeth, pointed out that, while the USAF could accept F-111s that might need extensive rework, Australia was a long way off and "would face tremendous difficulties".

The first F-111C was flown by GD in July 1968 and was formally accepted two months later. It was then completely dismantled by the USAF and, with the

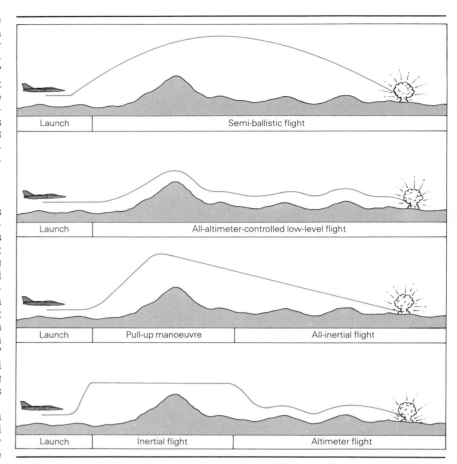

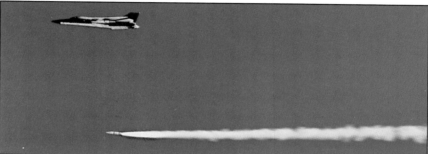

Above: Release of SRAM at low level over White Sands Missile Range.

Left: Simplified outlines of SRAM trajectories, showing the inherent versatility of this neat weapon. Moreover, these ignore the complete flexibility available in the horizontal direction followed.

Right: Another SRAM shot, this time from an FB at medium altitude.

other 23, put into long-term storage. Avionics were carefully packed into a thermostatically controlled hangar at Fort Worth. Wings were stacked inside the GD plant, while the fuselages, largely gutted of engines and equipment, rested on their wheels at Carswell AFB.

The usually decisive Aussies found the F-111 hard to handle. The Defence Minister, Malcolm Fraser, announced on December 5, 1969, he had formally asked the USAF to reactivate the 24 F-111C aircraft "so that they can be taken over by the RAAF as soon as possible". In the same month the wing parted from an F-111A and the situation was worse than before. The F-111Cs were actually the only F-111s in existence in 1969 that were never subjected to a static proof test, despite the intense concern of the Australians with structural integrity. It was not until March 14, 1973 that another Defence Minister, Lance H. Barnard, announced that the Australian government was going ahead with the F-111, and that the first F-111C would be accepted by its RAAF crew at Nellis on the following day.

In fact, the flow of aircrew to Nellis, broken off five years previously, had resumed in January 1973, and eventually the whole force of 24 aircraft were ferried via McClellan AFB (California), Hickham AFB (Hawaii), and either Pago Pago (American Samoa) or Nadi (Fiji),

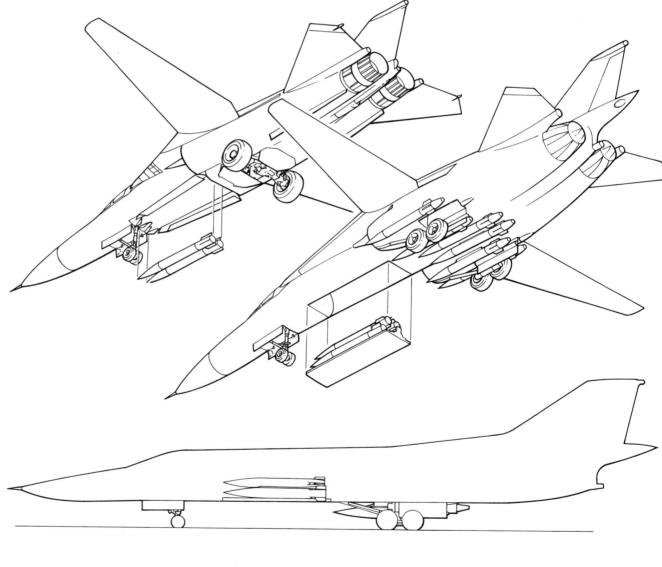

Above: The proposed stretched bomber version would have been powered by two GE F101 engines and carried eight SRAMs without using the wing pylons, and would have been able to fly missions over a radius extended to more than 2,600 miles (4,185 km).

Left: Partly for reasons of money the RAAF has been unable to think in strategic terms. Armourers of 482 Maintenance Sqn get 24 Snakeye bombs aboard each F-111C.

Above: Three aircraft of 6 Sqn curve in over the Gold Coast – as they call this bit of Queensland – homeward bound to Amberley, about 50 miles inland.

in four groups of six in the course of 1973. The first six arrived at Amberley on June 1, 1973. The much-loved Phantoms were returned, batches of six and five (one was lost in Australia) going back in 1972 and two final batches of six on June 6 and 20, 1973, to allow 1 and 6 Sqns to re-equip. The second group of six F-111Cs arrived at Amberley on July 27, and the third and fourth groups in September and November. Once Nos 1 and 6 Sqns were at last in business, forming No 82 (Strike) Wing, most of the political acrimony faded into history.

The One-Elevens settled into a training routine which takes them as far as Butterworth (Malaysia), Hawaii and even the USA, with various trips to Indonesia and other south-east Asian countries. The official figure for final capital cost was A$324 million, roughly four times the original 'ceiling' price quoted.

Australian service

In service the C has proved adequate in almost all respects, and 21,000 hours were flown before the first was lost on April 28, 1977. The pilot was a USAF officer on exchange posting, and it was said he only settled an old score as an RAAF pilot ejected from a USAF One-Eleven in 1973. Subsequently three further RAAF aircraft were lost; each was replaced by an ex-USAF F-111A purchased at what was said to be a price of A$5·95 million agreed in 1969 and not subsequently altered.

Like the USAF the RAAF now inevitably has a mix, in this case 16 Cs and four As. Further lack of standardization has followed the introduction after ex-

actly 20 years of study of the reconnaissance pallet. The final decision to continue with the removable multi-sensor package was taken by Defence Minister Barnard in December 1974, when a US$280,000 contract was placed with GD for a study to determine the work required to modify four aircraft. After some discussion, particularly over

Below: Liftoff of the first RAAF F-111C in GD hands at Fort Worth in April 1979. Inset: customer inspection of first RF installation.

prices and offsets, GD went ahead with a complete pallet mounting cameras, optical sights, IR linescan and a TV system, with sensor controls and displays in the right-hand cockpit. An F-111C flew to Fort Worth in late 1978 and was rolled out on 18 April 1979 for flight testing by GD and RAAF crews. By 1980 three further kits had been shipped to Amberley for installation by personnel of 452 Sqn, who look after the aircraft assigned to 1 and 6 Sqns (No 6 has the four convertible F/RF aircraft).

The RAAF's aircraft have increasingly been tasked with maritime and anti-ship missions. If funds can be made available it seems likely that an anti-ship missile will be purchased, and it is known that evaluations have been made of Harpoon, Exocet and Sea Eagle, and probably of other weapons in this category.

To return to the FB-111A force of SAC, it is only natural that, as with the B-58 before it, GD should have been active in canvassing advanced or stretched versions. By far the most important was a substantially enlarged model for SAC, which was discussed

from the mid-1970s and finally began to firm up as the FB-111H in 1977. Powered by two GE F101 engines, the same as then planned for the B-1, the H would have had a largely new fuselage, tandem-wheel main gears freeing the belly for weapons, and many other major and minor changes. It had the full support of everyone in the USAF from David C. Jones, Chief of Staff, down. Cost of rebuilding 65 FB-111As was put at $2·3 billion. Congressional approval was not forthcoming, so what happened next was a scaled-down plan of Sep-

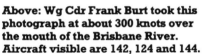

Above: Wg Cdr Frank Burt took this photograph at about 300 knots over the mouth of the Brisbane River. Aircraft visible are 142, 124 and 144.

tember 1979 to rebuild 66 FB-111As and 89 F-111Ds (essentially the surviving force of each type) to a rather lower standard called FB-111B/C, the B being the rebuilt FB and the C the rebuilt D. These would have had greater commonality with the existing aircraft, but F101 engines, more fuel and completely revised avionics and weapons would have turned them into very effective penetrators. Inflation, however, made the price of this reduced programme soar to $6·5 billion, or more than $40 million per aircraft and far more than the original estimated cost of a whole programme for 1,704 F-111s in 1963!

The FB-111B/C likewise never got the go ahead, and all that the USAF has so far been able to do is find $300 million for a programme to upgrade 65 FB-111As to improve their equipment. The Air Force Air Logistics Center at Sacramento began work in 1980 to add the Afsatcom (Air Force satellite communication system) terminal for sending and receiving teletype messages whilst airborne in any part of the world to effect a great improvement in operational readiness. A stall-warning system had been deemed urgent enough to be added, as well as the ALR-62/ALQ-137 mix described in an earlier chapter. At almost $5 million per aircraft, this modest avionics fit, which could just about fit into a Jeep, compares in price with that of a new F-111A. There is no plan at present to fit the AGM-86B ALCM, which in principle could be carried on the four wing pylons.

Left: Fortunately the Australian procurement of the F-111C is at present unique in human experience! For just under five years the whole force was dismantled and stored: here the fuselages are packed like sardines in a hangar at Carswell AFB.

The EF-111 Electric Fox

The air defence system encountered over North Vietnam, with its combination of SAMs, ground-controlled interceptors and radar-directed AAA based on a comprehensive network of surveillance radars, and consideration of the even more sophisticated system deployed by the Warsaw Pact, belatedly led the USAF to consider the need for a specialized tactical electronic warfare aircraft. Luckily, a suitable combination was found in the form of the ALQ-99 tactical jamming system used in the US Navy's EA-6B Prowler and the F-111A airframe: even so, it was to take another 15 years before the first EF-111A 'Electric Fox' was in service.

This final chapter dealing with a One-Eleven for the inventory describes a version far removed from anything contemplated in SOR-183, one whose purpose is not to carry traditional weapons but weapons of a purely electronic kind. As far back as 1942 the RAF was flying aircraft in the face of the enemy purely in order to find out about his emitters (ground and airborne radars, navaids and communications) and to interfere with them. Today the EF-111A is the newest and most advanced aircraft in the West carrying on this vital work.

Of course, any air force that takes its job seriously fits all its combat aircraft with EW (electronic warfare) systems. RWRs (radar warning receivers) are carried to indicate when the aircraft is being illuminated by a hostile radar, and advanced equipments give details about the illumination and perhaps even identify the type of radar and indicate its exact location. ECM (electronic countermeasures) may then be brought into play if the threat seems serious.

Powerful jammers can blanket the enemy wavelength(s), either by a 'brute force and ignorance' method in which the jammer simply has greater power (which is difficult, because small emitters in fighters can hardly overpower giant radars on the ground), or by deceptive techniques, involving sending out just the right signals in the right directions at the right times to stop the enemy radar from getting a good lock on. At the same time, small jammers can be ejected in dispensed cartridges, along with hot flares to defeat IR (heat) homing missiles. By far the commonest ECM of all is chaff, small slivers of reflective foil or aluminized film, which when dispensed in large clouds form a barrier that ordinary radars cannot penetrate.

Despite all this, modern airspace is becoming so perilous that even the latest tactical aircraft may not have a

Above: A salvaged F-111A is mounted on its side and subjected to giant electromagnetic pulses for the EF-111A programme.

very good chance of penetrating it deeply and surviving. This is particularly true of the airspace over the countries of the Warsaw Pact in eastern Europe, where the overall anti-air defence system is by far the strongest in the world. In several areas a NATO aircraft penetrating at a height of 10,000ft (3,000m) could be caught in the beams of 1,000 surface-based radars simultaneously. Behind this dense electronic barrier are the world's greatest concentration of rapid-fire guns, SAMs of many kinds and high-performance manned interceptors. Consequently, an attacking aircraft needs all the extra

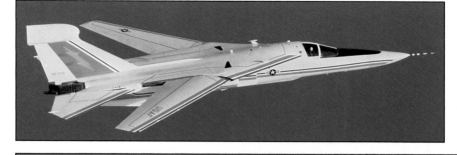

Left: The first prototype, 66-049, which was aerodynamically but, at this time, not electronically representative of the definitive EF.

Below: This photograph of the rather gaudy first EF, 66-049, was taken at Grumman's Calverton, NY, facility in June 1978.

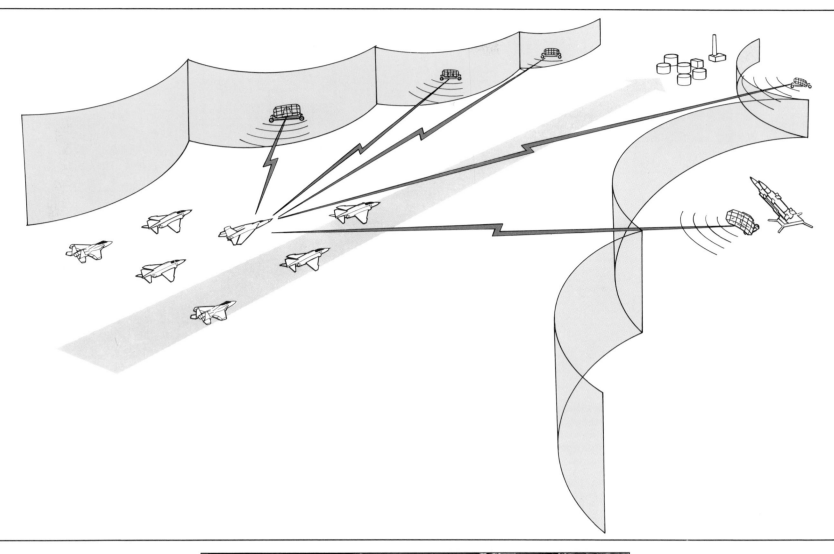

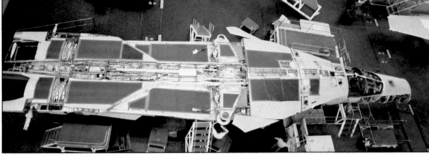

help it can get in order to have at least a reasonable chance of surviving.

Some two decades earlier the recognition that North Vietnam was beginning to construct electronic anti-air defence led to the urgent re-introduction of dedicated EW aircraft. The USAF completely rebuilt B-66 bombers and turned them into various species of EB-66, while the Navy did the same thing with F3D Skyknight interceptors and turned them into EF-10Bs. The Navy went on to buy much better purpose-designed EW aircraft, first the EA-6A Intruder and then the EA-6B Prowler, but the Air Force dragged its feet.

Urgent updating

Throughout the first half of the 1960s specialist agencies in the Air Force, and many experienced officers, grew increasingly alarmed as nothing appeared to be happening to counter the swiftly growing anti-air network facing the NATO air forces. Lieutenant-General Robert C. Mathis, Vice-Commander of the giant AFSC (Air Force Systems Command), said "In southeast Asia long-range Soviet radars detected our aircraft from gear-up to their attack run". He said a total updating of the USAF airborne EW capability was urgently needed "to support the tactical strike forces worldwide with high-power steerable, directional ECM jamming against early-warning, heightfinder, GCI (ground-control intercept) and acquisition radars".

It was one of the many times that, by default, the mighty USAF had let itself get into a situation that can fairly be called a crisis, and it was saved only by the sheer chance that it did not have to do any actual fighting. When it is realized that 15 years elapsed from the first move to update its pathetically inadequate EW capability in 1967 to the time that the first new EW aircraft became fully operational in 1982 the magnitude of the problem is thrown into focus. Politicians still like to imagine that

Centre above: An unserviceable F-111A mounted in the Grumman anechoic chamber for testing its electromagnetic compatibility.

Above: Fully instrumented 66-041 airborne in late 1978 after a year of generally very successful testing of the on-board systems and ALQ-99E.

Above: A grossly simplified portrayal of the way an EF-111A is intended to roll back the coverage of hostile air-defence radars and communications.

Left: This is the state to which the incoming F-111As are reduced in the Grumman teardown section (Station A) prior to rebuilding as an EF-111A.

peacetime deficiencies can somehow be put right in time of crisis by working around the clock for a few days. To get the Electric Fox took 15 years, and that was only possible because it was based on an existing tactical jamming system (ALQ-99) and an existing airframe (the F-111A).

Back in 1967 there were no EW tactical support aircraft in the Air Force except the EB-66s and a few EB-57s. All were ineffective electronically and overaged as aircraft, and it was planned to phase out the last in 1970. A new system was needed, as several lone voices had been explaining since 1963, but one always has to go through the motions of 'saving money' by studying lash-ups and interim stop-gaps, and by 1968 a lot of money had been spent on the ITEWS (interim tactical EW system) which was a proposal to re-equip, re-engine and re-wing the EB-66s.

As anyone could have predicted without charging the taxpayer a cent, this proved to be costly and impracticable, besides leaving the Air Force with an aircraft totally inadequate to meet the growing threat. So the next study, in 1968-70, focussed on a straightforward buy of Navy EA-6B Prowlers. This aircraft, the standard EW platform aboard Navy carriers until at least the year 2000, packages the powerful and properly designed ALQ-99 system into an A-6 Intruder airframe stretched to accommodate two extra crew, with the jamming emitters carried externally in up to five underwing and centreline pods, each with its own ram-air windmill to generate electric power.

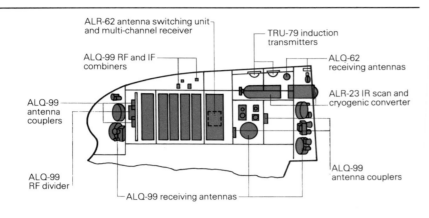

ALR-62 antenna switching unit and multi-channel receiver

ALQ-99 RF and IF combiners

ALQ-99 antenna couplers

ALQ-99 RF divider

ALQ-99 receiving antennas

TRU-79 induction transmitters

ALQ-62 receiving antennas

ALR-23 IR scan and cryogenic converter

ALQ-99 antenna couplers

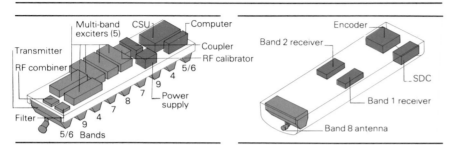

Multi-band exciters (5)

CSU

Computer

Coupler

RF calibrator

Transmitter

RF combiner

Filter

Power supply

Bands

Encoder

Band 2 receiver

SDC

Band 1 receiver

Band 8 antenna

Top: Major elements housed in the fin-tip pod, which weighs 370lb (168kg) and contains 583lb (264kg) of electronic receivers.

Above left: Simplified outline of items mounted on the equipment pallet in the weapon bay. Transmitter aerials emit through the 'canoe' radome.

Above left centre: The main pallet in the weapon bay door weighs 4,738lb (2,149kg) of which 4,274lb (1,939kg) comprises ALQ-99E avionic boxes.

Above: The pilot's side of the EF cockpit is not very different from an updated F-111A, which is hardly surprising; differences are at right.

Below: A comprehensive diagram of locations of external receiver and emitter aerials (antennas in the US) of the standard EF-111A.

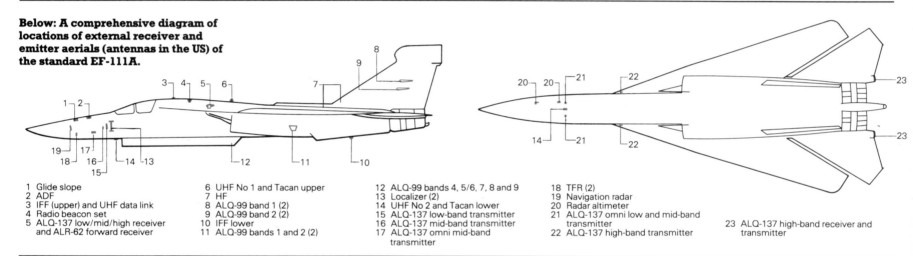

1 Glide slope	6 UHF No 1 and Tacan upper	12 ALQ-99 bands 4, 5/6, 7, 8 and 9
2 ADF	7 HF	13 Localizer (2)
3 IFF (upper) and UHF data link	8 ALQ-99 band 1 (2)	14 UHF No 2 and Tacan lower
4 Radio beacon set	9 ALQ-99 band 2 (2)	15 ALQ-137 low-band transmitter
5 ALQ-137 low/mid/high receiver	10 IFF lower	16 ALQ-137 mid-band transmitter
and ALR-62 forward receiver	11 ALQ-99 bands 1 and 2 (2)	17 ALQ-137 omni mid-band
		transmitter

18 TFR (2)	23 ALQ-137 high-band receiver and
19 Navigation radar	transmitter
20 Radar altimeter	
21 ALQ-137 omni low and mid-band	
transmitter	
22 ALQ-137 high-band transmitter	

The EA-6B does a good job, but it is open to criticism. The Air Force faulted it because it lacks supersonic performance, though it is arguable how often such performance would be needed in practice. Certainly, on some missions the EW aircraft has to fly in company with the attacking force, but with an external bombload no attack aircraft can fly much faster than an EA-6B, and the Navy has not often wished for greater speed.

A second criticism of the USAF was lack of range. This again is arguable. Like other A-6s the EA-6B has 15,940lb (7,230kg) of internal fuel, and depending on how many jammer pods are carried it can add to this up to four large drop tanks, so it could not be too heavily criticized on this score and certainly could fly useful tactical overland missions. On the other hand, it cannot equal the exceptional fuel capacity of the One-Eleven, nor the latter's high speed in the clean condition. The final black mark against the EA-6B was high price, but again this is relative and in fact is probably lower than for the EF-111A, though as it is impossible to compare a new-build aircraft with a rebuild such an assertion is of little value. One suspects there was also a bit of reluctance to accept a Navy aircraft, and a far from new one at that.

What seemed a better alternative was to try to package the TJS (tactical jamming system) of the EA-6B into the F-111. There was little chance of getting the F-111 production run extended, though this possibility was examined at length. The only alternative was to convert existing F-111s, and though the USAF later described these as 'surplus', all One-Elevens are actually pretty useful and converting a substantial number inevitably meant withdrawing the oldest and least effective examples from the inventory of Tactical Air Command. In fact almost exactly half of TAC's F-111A force were earmarked for conversion.

Fortunate coincidence
It is partly a matter of chance that it was found possible to convert the F-111A into an outstanding EW platform. Though said at the time to be not only cost-effective but also the lowest-risk solution, Grumman Aerospace, prime contractor for the EA-6B to the Navy and brought into the USAF programme at the very outset, was initially by no means certain the conversion could be done. Fitting two extra seats would have cut into the internal fuel because there were reasons why it was not desirable to extend the F-111 forward fuselage. Grumman received a Phase 1A contract in 1974, by which time it had already carried out deep study of an EW F-111, and in January 1975 an $85.9 million contract was received for the conversion of two F-111As into prototype EF-111As.

In addition to the hostile radars listed earlier a modern TJS aircraft has to counter the AI (airborne interception) radars of interceptors and IFF (identification friend or foe) systems. It can do this in various ways, and in most scenarios the USAF will also use Wild Weasel F-4Gs with Harm and other anti-radar missiles, as well as EW equipment such as ALQ-131 or ASPJ pods on each of the fighter or attack aircraft in the theatre. The powerful EW platforms can orbit well back from the battlefront, along with the TR-1 recon platforms, Awacs platforms and tankers. Here they would normally operate at high altitude, screening all air activity on the friendly side from hostile radars in what is called the Barrier Standoff role, with jamming tuned to the enemy's early warning, GCI, height-finding and target-acquisition radars and his IFF systems. In roughly similar locations they can also operate in the AI-jam role, with emissions tuned to obliterate the AI radars of enemy interceptors and thus further protect the aircraft on the friendly side.

Alternatively, the EF-111A can orbit closer to the enemy, either in the CAS (close air support) role, flying at low altitude to jam mobile battlefield radars for SAMs and AAA, or in the BAI (battlefield air interdiction) role, flying at medium level to jam all SAM/AAA radars as well as communications and data links. Finally, the EF can fly penetration escort missions accompanying

Left: A general view of the cockpit used by Grumman for development purposes, without ejection seats, with all wiring and panels installed.

Left below: Schematic diagram of the main front panel of the EF-111A with major items identified.

attacking aircraft on deep penetration strikes into hostile territory. It was clearly essential to select an aircraft able to accompany not only existing USAF attack aircraft but also those likely to enter the inventory during the remainder of this century, and at maximum weight an EF-111A can maintain 507 knots (584mph/940km/h) at low level over enemy territory. This is considerably slower than a clean One-Eleven in the nuclear role, but is considered adequate by the USAF.

As in the EA-6B the EF-111A carries its sensitive receiver subsystem in a large fairing on top of the fin. Six spiral antennae (aerials) are arranged looking to all points of the compass 60deg azimuth apart. They give full coverage of all threat frequencies, and indicate LOS (line of sight) to each emitter. The information they collect is used to manage the high-power jamming subsystem, prime contractor for which (under overall Grumman management) is Eaton's AIL Division at Deer Park, NY. In the EA-6B an IBM 4-pi computer manages a distributed external jamming system hung on pylons, as noted previously, but in the EF-111A ten powerful jammers are mounted on a large pallet housed in the weapon bay and radiating through a 16ft (4.9m) 'canoe' radome along the underside of the fuselage.

Smart jammer

ALQ-99 was thus a 'smart' (computer controlled) jammer from its inception in 1965. Its features included individual CW transmitters with higher than 1kW continuous power; high-gain aerials giving ERP (effective radiated power) in the megawatt range; closed-loop jammer control (for example, if a threat ceases emitting, the ALQ-99 instantly ceases to jam it); millisec (thousandth of a second) look-through to study the hostile emissions while jamming is in progress; real-time signal processing by the computer, which also handles BIT (built-in test) and fault isolation; and EMC (electromagnetic compatibility) testing of the complete radiating aircraft in a giant anechoic chamber to confirm that the massive jamming emissions would not interfere with or damage the aircraft's own delicate avionics.

In 1970–73 the XCAP (expanded capability) ALQ-99A came into use on the EA-6B. This offered doubled frequency coverage, greater computer capacity, new wide-band transmitters, a recording capability for future threat analysis, a new Raytheon multimode exciter giving many new features including track-breaking and CFAR (constant false-alarm rate) jamming, and a lot of new computer software. Next, in 1974, came ICAP (increased capability) ALQ-99D, with digital tuning to exact frequencies; a multi-format cockpit display and keyboard; peripheral processor; a faster encoder and 8-MHz clock; broad-beam jamming aerials and further improved software to speed up response in the auto mode; and an expanded frequency sector mode, jamming individual threats.

These considerable improvements

1 Auxiliary brake handle
2 Landing gear control panel
3 Arresting hook handle
4 External stores jettison button
5 Agent discharge/Fire detect test switch
6 Fuselage fire pushbutton warning lamp
7 Engine fire pushbutton warning lamps
8 Angle-of-attack indexer
9 Wing sweep flap/slat position indicator
10 Engine tachometers
11 Engine turbine inlet temperature indicators
12 Engine fuel flow indicators
13 Engine nozzle position indicators
14 Engine pressure ratio indicators
15 Hydraulic pressure indicators
16 Engine oil pressure indicators
17 Control surface position indicator
18 True airspeed indicator
19 Horizontal situation indicator
20 Airspeed Mach indicator
21 Attitude director indicator
22 Altitude vertical velocity indicator
23 Threat indicator
24 Standby airspeed indicator
25 Left status indicator
26 Self-contained attitude indicator
27 Standby vertical velocity indicator
28 Radar altimeter indicator

29 Right status indicator
30 Fuselage fuel quantity indicator
31 Fuel quantity indicator test button
32 Landing gear position indicator lamps
33 Instrument system coupler control
34 Total/select fuel quantity indicator

35 Takeoff trim indicator lamp
36 Takeoff trim button
37 Fuel quantity indicator select knob
38 Main caution lamp panel
39 Lower caution lamp panel

40 ILS control panel
41 Ram doors/oil quantity panel
42 Annunciator indicator
43 Standby altimeter
44 Master caution lamp
45 Magnetic compass
46 TFR scope panel

47 Nav radar scope panel
48 UHF radio control panel
49 TTWS control indicator panel
50 Inertial nav control panel
51 Stores jettison select panel

52 Landing gear emergency release handle
53 JSS/SPS warning and caution panel
54 Angle-of-attack indexer
55 Clock
56 Digital display indicator

57 Jammer status panel
58 JSS modes select panel
59 Disposables control panel
60 Digital display indicator control panel
61 Stowage bag

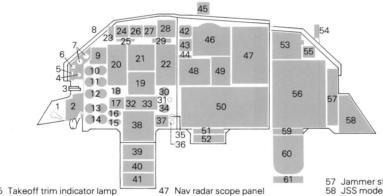

Above: Main cooling-air outlets at the rear of the pallet from which hot air blasts while ALQ-99E is operating. The rear of the radome can be seen.

Left: Close-up of the fin-tip pod on 66-041 after delivery to Mountain Home AFB. There is little hint of the complex array of internal receivers.

Left: A fin and pod for an EF-111A in the Canadair plant at Montreal. This section posed structural as well as aerodynamic and avionic problems.

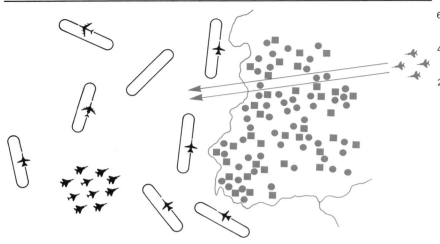

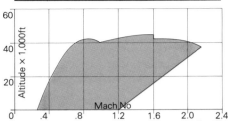

Above: Simplified representation of the barrier standoff and AI jammer roles which will be flown by the EF-111A to protect friendly aircraft.

Right: In the penetration escort role the EFs would accompany the friendly attacking aircraft (here depicted as F-4s) throughout hostile airspace.

Below: The close-in role demands that the EF-111A should fly racetrack patterns at different heights close to the edge of hostile airspace. At the same time, other EF-111As orbiting at higher altitudes would guard supporting aircraft against attacks by enemy interceptors.

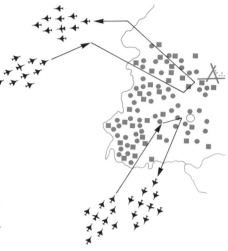

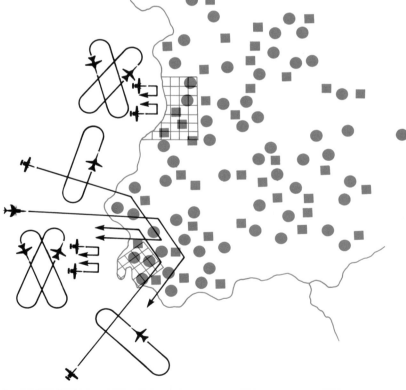

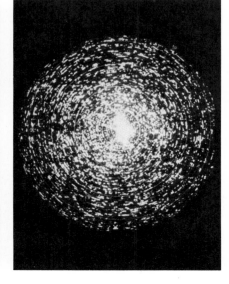

Above: The EF-111A performance envelope is essentially the same as that of other F-111 versions, though Mach 1.2 at sea level would be rare.

Above: The first EF delivered to TAC was the twice-rebuilt 66-041, seen here with MO tail code after arrival at Mountain Home in January 1982.

not only enabled the ALQ-99 installation to handle more hostile threats faster, but also opened the way to the desired system for the EF-111A which, by virtue of increased automation and further improved software, enables one man to do what in the EA-6B takes three. The system is the ALQ-99E, developed in 1974–78. Apart from the single-operator computer control it features inflight-adaptable aerials; a new multiband, multispot exciter with its own modulation microprocessor; digital CFAR jamming; and complete isolation of active and passive systems, the latter comprising the ALR-62 (V)-4 TTWS (terminal threat warning subsystem), as well as the active ALQ-137 (V)-4 SPS (self-protection subsystem). Thus, to recapitulate, the main JSS (jamming subsystem), the ALQ-99E detects, identifies, locates, records and jams every kind of hostile emitter using computer control to give high-power jamming with highly effective signal modulations in just the right directions and at precisely the right times. It is universally considered the best EW system in the world at present.

Turning an F-111A into an EF is a major rebuild operation, but as far as possible it preserves the F-111's basic flight qualities and manoeuvre envelope. Thanks to the prior exhaustive test programme the basic airframe has a 10,000-hour life, and this is also the life put on all new structure added in producing an EF. The F-111A airframes typically had about 2,000 hours when they were grounded for conversion, and it is calculated that at normal peacetime utilization the remaining 8,000 hours will take them up to about the year 2010, possibly with occasional local rework.

New equipment
The main changes are the fin receivers and installation of the jamming equipment pallet. Canadair supplies the fin, which is reinforced to carry 370lb (168kg) of pod structure loaded with 583lb (264kg) of internal electronics (see diagram). Grumman assembles the main jammer installation, which mounted on its pallet weighs 4,274lb (1,939kg), while the canoe radome and door adds a further 464lb (210kg). Thus it is generally agreed that, not surprisingly, the EF flies like an F-111A with a 6,000lb (2,700kg) bombload, though as most of the extra weight is internal the rate of roll is perhaps a bit better. On Red Flag and other exercises EFs have repeatedly demonstrated their ability to fly formation with other F-111s making high-speed attacks.

The rebuilding of the fin and weapons bay are by no means all the airframe changes involved. As the jamming

Left: Actual photographs showing the screen of a ground air-defence surveillance radar (far left) with the normal unjammed picture; when the receiver is jammed by transmissions from the airborne ALQ-99E it becomes impossible to decipher the radar returns (near left).

system is internal it cannot use ram-air windmill generators, and a new EPS (electric power system) is needed. The original 60-kVA IDGs (integrated-drive generators) on the engines are replaced by large machines rated at 90 kVA, supplying the jamming pallet via a completely new rewired electrical subsystem. Rewiring is partly responsible for reducing weight by 1,600lb (726kg). At least as important as the installation of two new ECS (environmental control system) installations, the air-cycle system used in the F-111F, with a ram inlet under the front of the right-hand main engine inlet duct, and a liquid (Coolanol) refrigeration system to provide cold air at 40deg F (4.4deg C) to cool the high-power avionics which, being internal, have no slipstream cooling. The liquid system rejects heat overboard via two RAHEs (ram-air heat exchangers) located at the roots of both tailplanes. Another local modification is the addition of a blade aerial on the right side of the fuselage under the wing trailing edge, and flush skin aerials in both glove leading edges.

Prototype testing
In 1974–76 Grumman Aerospace at Calverton, the USAF Rome Air Development Center and Kirtland AFB used five prototype or early production F-111A aircraft in exploring radiative patterns, EMC and nuclear hardness with giant electronic pulses. On December 15, 1975, Grumman began a 29-flight programme at Calverton with an F-111A fitted with a dummy canoe aerial to check basic flight performance and handling. It was followed on March 10, 1977, by the first of the two EF-111A prototypes funded in 1975. This aircraft, gaily painted 66-049, was aerodynamically representative of the definitive aircraft, with the fin pod and other modifications, but did not have a fully operative jamming system. An almost complete operative system was flown on the second prototype, 66-041, painted in the low-visibility pale grey of the production aircraft and flown from Calverton on May 17, 1977.

Subsequent testing confirmed predicted aircraft performance and handling, and generally excellent jamming effect (on one occasion a New England ANG unit called up to request that jamming be switched off so that it could find out where its own aircraft were). A minor redesign of the fin was called for and there were just over 200 other snags, mainly in the area of reliability and maintainability, all speedily corrected to the point where in 1979 direct maintenance was averaging an impressive 20 man-hours per flight hour, less than that required for regular F-111s. Totally Blue Suit (ie, by Air Force personnel) follow-on testing began in April 1979 and was completed in October after 261 hours in 86 flights. Reliability and maintenance easily bettered all targets, despite severe surge demands and sustained high sortie rates, all in the hands of the 366th TFW at Mountain Home AFB assisted by

Above: A superb study of 66-019, the third production EF, after delivery to Mountain Home.

personnel from Eglin AFB's Tactical Air Warfare Center.

Particularly bearing in mind the patchy record of the basic One-Eleven for reliability – described by a USAF spokesman at Mountain Home during EF testing as "not enviable" – it is especially gratifying to record that the complex and challenging EF is not only much better than the unmodified aircraft but considerably better than the USAF's requirements. As a result, in November 1979 the DSARC (Defense Systems Acquisition Review Council) breathed a sigh of relief and lifted all production constraints. Grumman has since been in production with conversion kits, with an average of six airframes at Calverton at any one time.

Production Lot I consisted of one aircraft – the completely refurbished 66-049 – which was rolled out at Calverton on June 19, 1981. This was the first time anyone had seen the definitive production cockpit, which has only one set of flight controls and a very neat set of displays for the EWO in the right seat. This aircraft vanished into Grumman's anechoic chamber for additional EMC testing, and the first example actually delivered to TAC was 66-041, likewise completely brought up to production standard and delivered to the 366th TFW 17 months behind schedule in November 1981. This was the first of the two aircraft in Lot II, while Lot III comprised four aircraft, all delivered in 1982. Lot IV included eight aircraft delivered by the late summer of 1983, and

IOC (initial operational capability) was to be achieved in November 1983. Lot V, comprising 12 aircraft, was in the Grumman plant in 1983 and were then all due for delivery by September 1984. The final batch, Lot VI, comprises 15 aircraft due for delivery at monthly intervals between September 1984 and November 1985. Originally all were to have been in use before 1983.

In service six Electric Foxes – which seems a better name than the pretentious Electronic Warrior favoured by the

Below: Another Electric Fox, 66-013, showing the overall remarkably clean appearance of this extremely capable jamming platform.

Air Force – are being held for training and attrition, while 24 are assigned to the 388th Electronic Combat Squadron at Mountain Home and 12 to a second ECS at RAF Upper Heyford. The aircraft based in Britain will clearly be those 'at the sharp end' in the immediate future. One of the most severe problems has been trying to find a friendly block of airspace with any kind of air defence system rivalling that in Warsaw Pact countries. Nothing like this exists anywhere in NATO, and virtually all the really tough evaluation of how the EF will perform against dense emitter concentrations has been done on simulators, notably those at Calspan's REDCAP facility in Buffalo.

There is every reason to believe that this potentially outstanding aircraft would in practice perform as advertised, though it is extremely hard to demonstrate this in advance. Eventually it will have JTIDS (Joint Tactical Information Distribution System) terminals with which it will be able to plug in in real time to ground bases or to an Awacs aircraft, both to protect the latter more effectively and to feed Elint (electronic intelligence) information as fast as it is collected. Certainly the only big problem with the EFs is their rather limited numbers, which will mean that combat losses will at least temporarily leave significant gaps in a particularly vital part of the inventory.

Experimental Variants

As well as enabling it to penetrate hostile airspace at low levels and high speeds, the One-Eleven's swing wings offer unique opportunities for aeronautical research, allowing wings of various configurations to be tested at any required sweep angle. Since 1970 NASA has exploited these opportunities in a series of programmes investigating the technology of supercritical wings, which offer greater efficiency at high subsonic speeds. Most recently the F-111 has become the recipient of the uniquely flexible Mission Adaptive Wing, whose profile can be adjusted for any flight condition without the use of flaps or other drag-inducing devices.

From early in the TFX programme it was evident to such people as NASA's John Stack that the F-111 would be a uniquely valuable aircraft for R&D (research and development) purposes. Unlike previous aircraft it can test wings at any desired angle of sweepback, and in some programmes this is a considerable asset. But in the early 1960s NASA was more concerned with lunar exploration than with lift-drag ratios, and little was done for a further ten years, though NASA's aerodynamicists were hard at work.

Probably the single most important advance in subsonic and transonic wing technology in the past 25 years is the so-called supercritical wing, which compared with a classic wing is much thicker (around 17 per cent thickness/chord ratio), having a bluff leading edge and almost an upside-down profile, with a flatter top and more bulging camber on the underside. It sounds like an absurd idea, and the only reason it might appear to give lift upward instead of downward is that the trailing edge is curved gently downward, so at least the air comes off the wing with some downward momentum. In fact it is a brilliant idea, because the air over the upper surface is less violently accelerated and thus the wing can be driven to a higher airspeed before it encounters sonic speed at the line of peak suction on the upper surface, with its attendant shockwaves and high drag.

Supercritical wings in practice are not so much used to make aeroplanes go faster as to enable them to fly at the same speed with greater efficiency. The supercritical wing can be made so much deeper that the skins can be thinner and the weight much less. Compared with a normal thin wing the aspect ratio (the slenderness in plan form) can be greatly enhanced, giving greater efficiency in subsonic cruising flight. There is room for more fuel inside the wing, and the bluff leading edge improves takeoff and low-speed handling without the need for adding false bluffness with a Kruger flap. Altogether the supercritical wing has transformed the latest generation of large passenger jets and executive aircraft, though Rockwell's Columbus Division, which received NASA's original contract, has been unable to reap much business benefit.

Early applications

A rather imperfect supercritical wing flew under NASA contract on a T-2C Buckeye in November 1970, and on a NASA F-8 Crusader on March 9, 1971. By this time the USAF interest in the B-1 was beginning to trickle more money into the idea, and in early 1973 the 13th F-111A was assigned to test a supercritical wing at different sweep angles. Ostensibly part of NASA's TACT (Transonic Aircraft Technology) programme, aircraft 63-9778 was painted in the badges and initials of a remarkable lot of sponsors. For the USAF there was the AFFTC (Air Force Flight Test Center) and AFFDL (Flight Dynamics Lab). For

NASA there was the ARC (Ames Research Center), FRC (Dryden Flight Research Center) and LRC (Langley Research Center, where the F-111 had it earliest origins).

Curiously, instead of fitting a long slender wing, of the kind used on modern transports, the TACT wing fitted was blunt and of short span, with much reduced aspect ratio and broad-chord tips. Sweep angles were reduced to 10deg (min) and 58deg (max), and there was very marked washout (wing twist reducing AOA progressively from root to tip). Droop leading-edge flaps and area-increasing trailing-edge flaps were fitted, with roll spoilers well outboard. Prolonged test flying took place to give results evaluated against those measured previously in 24 NASA flights in the unmodified configuration. This programme, in 1965–68, provided a considerable amount of data, and for good measure one TF30 engine was also fitted with a new IPCS (integrated propulsion control system) which instead of the usual hydromechanical control used digital electronics to control the engine, its inlet and variable nozzle.

NASA and the USAF said little about the results of the supercritical wing programme, but continued tinkering with the wings and by summer 1979 had moved on to flying large wing gloves intended to provide what was called "natural laminar flow". Since 1949 many organizations have sought to fly an aircraft whose boundary layer, instead of being turbulent, was maintained in a

smooth laminar condition. This would significantly reduce drag, so that in 1953 Handley Page in England was rash enough to publish ideas for subsonic jetliners able to fly from Britain to Australia non-stop. Neither that company nor anyone else ever succeeded in building an aircraft in which laminar flow was truly practical. A fly on the leading edge will instantly result in a turbulent boundary layer, as will dirt, manufacturing imperfections and even an already turbulent atmosphere, but by 1979 NASA wished to see how far it would be possible to use the new technology of deep supercritical wings to maintain a favourable (accelerating) pressure gradient over most of the chord and thus preserve laminar flow by natural means, without any of the sucking or blowing of the previous active schemes. (Even this was not new, the deep Griffith aerofoil having been produced in 1945.)

First, the One-Eleven had to be flown without the use of any wing movables, and it was soon confirmed that at 10deg

Above: Another picture of 63-9778 in original TACT form, showing the fully instrumented wing with considerable wash-out of incidence from root to tip.

Above: Specially drawn for this book, this side elevation (profile) shows 63-9778 in its first rebuilt form with the original supercritical wing.

Right: The TACT aircraft with the wings in the intermediate sweep position. In fact, the wings are no more advanced than those of the A310 Airbus.

Opposite: In contast the attempt to achieve a large degree of 'natural' laminar flow was a major challenge. Note the added glove on each wing.

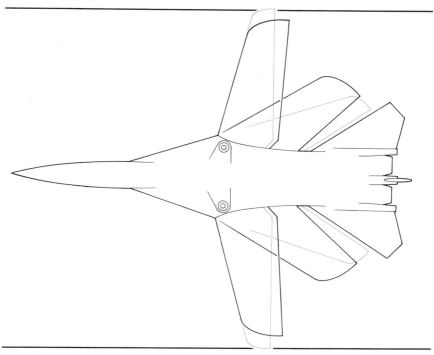

Above right: This version of a simple NASA drawing shows the low aspect-ratio plan shape of the supercritical wing superimposed on the original F-111 outline in blue.

sweep it was possible to take off and land without using droops or flaps. Large gloves were then built around the wings near mid-span, made with extremely accurate profile which then had to be slightly marred by adding instrumentation to measure surface pressures, pitot-rake ram pressures and other unknowns, such as where transition to a turbulent boundary layer actually took place. In all, 19 flights were made at heights up to 30,000ft (9,000m), at Mach numbers to 0.85 and with sweep restricted to 10–26deg. Again, no results have been published, though this does not necessarily mean that laminar flow has yet again proved an elusive pipe-dream.

Mission-Adaptive Wing
This was not to be the end of the road for the NASA/USAF One-Eleven. As part of the far-reaching AFTI (Advanced Fighter Technology Integration) programme the USAF wishes to investigate what is called the MAW, for Mission-Adaptive Wing. It is the logical next stage beyond today's crude rigid wings to which crude rigid slats, droops or flaps are hinged. Birds do it better: their wings can change shape in smooth curves exactly adapted to each flight condition. For many years aerodynamicists have wished to do the same, the only objection being that it is very difficult. Fortunately the AFFDL found $20 million, and a contract for a pair of almost totally new wings was awarded to, of all people, the losing TFX finalist, Boeing-Wichita.

Boeing had already devoted a lot of thought to how, and how far, it would be possible to replace crude wings by flexible ones. Indeed, as far back as 1969 the first 747 had flown with giant leading-edge flaps with skins largely made of glassfibre composite able to take up a strongly arched shape as they extend from the main surface. With the One-Eleven it was planned to go the whole hog and make the entire pivoted wing flexible apart from the original torsion box. The two boxes, stripped of their previous overlays and gloves, were removed from ship 778 and sent to Wichita in late 1981. Meanwhile, Boeing had already built a full-scale wing section to determine loads and stresses, structurally proved each component for the MAW, and also shown in tunnel

**Right: The Mission-adaptive wing in
model form set up for high-speed
tunnel test at the USAF Arnold
Engineering Development Center,
Tennessee.**
**Right below: The Boeing-Wichita
artist faced a challenge in trying to
produce a popular picture of the
MAW in action.**
**Foot of page: Far more informative is
this photograph of the left-hand
MAW at Boeing Military Airplane Co
in Seattle. Protractors are measuring
deflections prior to AFTI/F-111 flight.**

testing that the MAW might be expected to improve buffet-free lift by 69
per cent, sustained lift by 25 per cent
and reduce cruise drag by 6 per cent at
subsonic speeds and 7 per cent in
supersonic flight. A company spokesman said it could be "the single most
innovative development in years".

Design details changed slightly in
1980–82, but it has always been the
intention to maintain an unbroken
flexible upper skin from leading edge to
trailing edge, using basically a GRP
(glass-reinforced plastics) structure.
Prolonged studies appeared to show
that the compression of the underside in
the low-speed or manoeuvre regime
would cause buckling unless some form
of spanwise discontinuity was accepted,
allowing one part to slide over its neigh-
bour. The leading edge behaves as a
fully variable droop flap, driven by a
powered system from root to tip. The
trailing edge likewise is fully powered,
behaving as both ailerons (with asym-
metric flexure) and flaps (with sym-
metric flexure). Features include high
actuation power and rapid movement
when demanded, the objective being
trailing-edge rotation at 30deg/sec.

Test programme
Flight control modes to be tested include cruise camber control for peak
efficiency, manoeuvre load control for
quicker dogfight manoeuvres without
overstressing the wing root, and DLC
(direct lift control) to permit the pilot
either to change the aircraft longitudinal
pitch angle nose-up or nose-down without diving or climbing, or alternatively
to cause the aircraft to make sudden
movements in the vertical plane without
altering the pitch attitude at all. It should
also be possible to effect automatic
alleviation of gust loads to give passen-
gers (and structures) a smoother ride.

Naturally, the flight control system
with the MAW will be of the fully
redundant digital FBW (fly-by-wire)
type, coupled to a dual electro-hy-
draulic wing actuation system. In mid-
1983 it was expected that limiting leading-edge angle would be 15deg down,
while the trailing edge is expected to
move 4deg up and 19deg (the original
objective was 30deg) down. The programme has slipped by about a year
from the original objective of autumn
1982, but as this was written it was clear
that flight with the MAW wings under
manual control should be possible well
before the end of 1983. In 1984 it is
expected that fully automatic flight will
be possible, the pilot merely inserting
flight Mach number, altitude and
manoeuvre condition and leaving it to
the FCS (flight control system) digital
computer continuously to select the best
wing profile.

The F-111 wing has a reasonable
amount of internal room for the power
actuation system and linkages. Future
transports might have even more, but
from the viewpoint of the USAF prime
candidates for the MAW are the F-16
and other advanced fighters, and it
remains to be seen whether their small
wings will prove mission-adaptable.

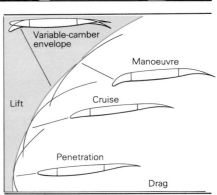

**Above: The thing that matters about
the MAW is not plan shape but the
variable section profile. Other
aircraft, such as the F-16, can pivot
leading and trailing edges, but only in
a crude way with hinged rigid
surfaces. The MAW is flexible.**

Glossary and abbreviations

AAA	Anti-aircraft artillery
AAM	Air-to-air missile
Active	Emitting radiation
ADF	Automatic direction finding system
Aerial	British word for antenna
AFB	US Air Force Base
AGL	Above ground level
AI	Airborne interception
Antenna	American word for aerial
AOA	Angle of attack
Aspect ratio	Wing slenderness in plan-form, numerically $span^2$/area
ASPJ	Advanced self-protection jammer
Awacs	Airborne warning and control system
Azimuth	Bearing, direction or angular rotation in horizontal plane
BG	Bomb Group
Bite	Built-in test equipment
BW	Bomb Wing
CAP	Combat air patrol
CAS	Close air support
CFAR	Constant false-alarm rate
CG	Centre of gravity
Chord	Distance across wing from leading to trailing edge measured parallel to longitudinal axis of fuselage
CNI	Communications, navigation, identification
CRT	Cathode-ray tube
CW	Continuous-wave radiation
DF	Direction finding
Digital	Operating with discrete on/off pulses or bits which instead of being measured are counted
DLI	Deck-launched intercept
DME	Distance measuring equipment
DoD	Department of Defense
Doppler	Radar which measures changes in frequency between reflections from ground ahead of and behind the aircraft, thus giving accurate measure of speed over the ground (doppler effect is also used to pick out moving targets)
ECCM	Electronic counter-countermeasures
ECM	Electronic countermeasures
EM	Electromagnetic
EO	Electro-optical
EW	Electronic warfare
FADF	Fleet Air Defense Fighter
FBW	Fly by wire, electrically signalled
FLIR	Forward-looking IR
FOD	Foreign-object damage
FOV	Field of view
G	Acceleration due to Standard Gravity, unit of linear acceleration
GCI	Ground-controlled interception
GD	General Dynamics Corporation
GE	General Electric Company (USA)
GHz	Gigahertz, thousands of millions of cycles per second
HAS	Hardened aircraft shelter
HE	High explosive
HF	High frequency
HUD	Head-up display
Hz	Hertz, cycles per second
I-band	EM radiation 8 to 10GHz
IFF	Identification friend or foe
ILS	Instrument landing system
INS	Inertial navigation system
IR	Infra-red, heat radiation
Iron bomb	Ordinary HE bomb
IRCM	IR countermeasures
IRWR	IR warning receiver
J-band	EM radiation 10 to 20GHz
Jammer	ECM emitter designed to smother hostile radars or radios
JTIDS	Joint tactical information distribution system
kHz	Kilohertz, thousands of cycles per second
kT	Kilotonnes yield
kVA	Kilovolt-amperes, unit of electrical power
kW	Kilowatt, unit of DC electrical power
Lantirn	Low-altitude navigation and targeting IR at night
LGB	Laser-guided bomb
Lo	As close to the Earth's surface as possible, typically 200 to 1,000ft (90–300m)
Mach	Unit of airspeed equal to the local speed of sound
MHz	Megahertz, millions of cycles per second
MTI	Moving-target indication
NACA	US National Advisory Committee for Aeronautics
NASA	US National Aeronautics and Space Administration
NIS	NATO identification system
nm	Nautical mile
OKB	Soviet experimental construction (ie, design) bureau
Passive	Not emitting
PD	Pulse doppler type of radar
Pod	Streamlined container carried externally
PPI	Plan position indication
PRF	Pulse-recurrence frequency (or repetition)
RAAF	Royal Australian Air Force
RAF	Royal Air Force
Raster	TV picture built up line-by-line
RCS	Radar cross-section
RDT&E	Research, development, test and evaluation
RHAWS	Radar homing and warning system
RMTS	Ranger and marked-target seeker
RTAFB	Royal Thai Air Force Base
RWR	Radar warning receiver
SAC	USAF Strategic Air Command
SAM	Surface-to-air missile
SAR	Synthetic-aperture radar
Semi-active	Homing on radiation reflected from a target illuminated by radar carried in fighter or some other vehicle (not the missile)
SecDef	US Secretary for Defense
SIF	Selective identification facility
Signature	Characteristic form of each emitter's radiation, forming a kind of fingerprint
Smart	Self-guided to home on an illuminated target, especially using laser radiation
Slick	Streamlined (Aero-1A shape) bomb
SOJ	Stand-off jammer
Solid-state	Based on semiconductor materials instead of vacuum tubes
SOR	Specific operational requirement
Span	Distance measured across tips of wings
STOL	Short takeoff and landing
TAC	USAF Tactical Air Command
Tacan	Tactical air navigation
Taileron	Tailplanes able to move together as primary control in pitch and opposite sense as control in roll (tailplane/aileron)
TF, TFR	TFR Terrain following, terrain-following radar
TFS	USAF Tactical Fighter Squadron
TFW	USAF Tactical Fighter Wing
TFX	Tactical fighter experimental
TI	Texas Instruments Inc
TJS	Tactical jamming system
TsAGI	Soviet central aero and hydrodynamics institute
Turbofan	Turbojet with oversize low-pressure compressor delivering excess airflow bypassing core of engine to add to jet downstream
UHF	Ultra-high frequency
USAF	US Air Force
USN	US Navy
VG	Variable geometry, especially variable sweepback
VHF	Very high frequency
V/STOL	Vertical or short takeoff and landing
Wing loading	Aircraft weight divided by wing area
WSO	Weapon-system officer (wizzo)

Specifications

	F-111A/E	F-111C	F-111D
Engine	TF30-P-3	TF30-P-3	TF30-P-9
Inlet	Triple Plow 1*	Triple Plow 1	Triple Plow 2
TO thrust	18,500lb/8,390kg	18,500lb/8,390kg	20,840lb/9,453kg
Wingspan 16°	63ft 0in/19.2m	70ft 0in/21.34m	63ft 0in/19.2m
Wingspan 72½°	31ft 11½in/9.74m	33ft 11½in/10.35m	31ft 11½in/9.740m
Wing area 16°	525sq ft/48.78sq m	550sq ft/51.1sq m	525sq ft/48.78sq m
Length	75ft 6½in/23.03m	75ft 6½in/23.03m	75ft 6½in/23.03m
Height	17ft 0½in/5.19m	17ft 0½in/5.19m	17ft 0½in/5.19m
Fuel (internal)	4,191gal/19,052lt	4,191gal/19,052lt	4,191gal/19,052lt
Fuel (external)	2,000gal/9,092lt	3,000gal/13,638lt	2,000gal/9,092lt
Weight empty	46,172lb/20,943kg	47,303lb/21,456kg	46,631lb/21,151kg
Weight max TO	91,300lb/41,400kg	110,000lb/49,900kg	100,000lb/45,360kg
Avionics			
Radar	APQ-113	APQ-113	APQ-130
TFR	APQ-110	APQ-110	APQ-128
Radar altimeter	APN-167	APN-167	APN-167
RHAWS	APS-109A	APS-109A	APS-109C
CMDS	ALE-28	ALE-28	ALE-28
CMRS	ALR-23	ALR-23	ALR-41
INS	AJQ-20A	AJQ-20A	AJN-16
Tacan	ARN-52	ARN-52	ARN-52(V)
ILS	ARN-58	ARN-58	ARN-58A
IFF (AIMS)	APX-64	APX-64	APX-64(V)
IFF	—	—	APX-76
Optical sight	ASG-23	ASG-23	AVA-9 (HUD)
Doppler	—	—	APN-189
Astrocompass	—	ASQ-119	—
ECM jammer	pods	pods	pods
SPS	—	—	—
TTWS	—	—	—

	F-111F	FB-111A	EF-111A
Engine	TF30-P-100	TF30-P-7	TF30-P-3
Inlet	Triple Plow 2	Triple Plow 2	Triple Plow 1
TO thrust	25,100lb/11,385kg	20,350lb/9,230kg	18,500lb/8,390kg
Wingspan 16°	63ft 0in/19.2m	70ft 0in/21.34m	63ft 0in/19.2m
Wingspan 72½°	31ft 11½in/9.74m	33ft 11½in/10.35m	31ft 11½in/9.74m
Wing area 16°	525sq ft/48.78sq m	550sq ft/51.1sq m	525sq ft/48.78sq m
Length	75ft 6½in/23.03m	75ft 7in/23.04m	76ft 0in/23.17m
Height	17ft 0½in/5.19m	17ft 0½in/5.19m	20ft 0in/6.1m
Fuel (internal)	4,184gal/19,020lt	4,673gal†/21,243lt	4,173gal/18,970lt
Fuel (external)	2,000gal/9,092lt	3,000gal/13,638lt	none
Weight empty	47,481lb/21,537kg	47,980lb/21,763kg	55,275lb/25,072kg
Weight max TO	100,000lb/45,360kg	119,243lb/54,088kg	89,000lb/40,370kg
Avionics			
Radar	APQ-144	APQ-114	APQ-160
TFR	APQ-146	APQ-134	APQ-110
Radar altimeter	APN-167	APN-167	APN-167
RHAWS	APS-109	APS-109B	—
CMDS	ALE-28	ALE-28	ALE-28
CMRS	ALR-41	ALR-41	ALR-23
INS	AJN-16	AJN-16	AJQ-20A
Tacan	ARN-52(V)	ARN-52(V)	ARN-52
ILS	ARN-58A	ARN-58A	ARN-58
IFF (AIMS)	APX-64(V)	APX-64(V)	APX-64
IFF	—	APX-78	—
Optical sight	ASG-27	ASG-25	—
Doppler	—	APN-185	—
Astrocompass	—	ASQ-119	—
ECM jammer	pods	pods	ALQ-99E
SPS	—	—	ALQ-137(V)4
TTWS	—	—	ALR-62(V)4

* F-111E, T Plow 2; † with bomb bay tanks (2)

Performance

All versions can briefly exceed Mach 2 (1,320mph, 2124 km/h) above 30,000ft (9144m) in clean condition and at MAX power (afterburner). At low levels the clean maximum is typically Mach 1.2 (912mph, 1468km/h), but the EF-111A is limited to about 500kt.

Deployment

F-111A 4520th Combat Crew Training Sqn, Nellis AFB, Las Vegas, Nevada; 4480th TFW, Nellis; 474th TFW, Nellis; 347th TFW, detached to Takhli RTAFB; today serving only with the 366th TFW, Mountain Home AFB, Boise, Idaho, and the 57th Fighter Weapons Wing, formerly McClellan AFB, now at Nellis. Support for all USAF One-Elevens by Sacramento Air Logistics Center, McClellan AFB, Sacramento, California.

F-111B Test programmes from NAS Patuxent River, Miramar, Point Mugu and Lakehurst, but never operational.

F-111C No 6 Sqn, RAAF, Amberley, Ipswich, Queensland.

F-111D 27 TFW, Cannon AFB, Clovis, New Mexico.

F-111E Briefly at Cannon, then 20th TFW, RAF Upper Heyford, Oxon.

F-111F 347th TFW, Mountain Home (and Takhli RTAFB and Taegu AB); 366th TFW, Mountain Home; now only with 48th TFW, RAF Lakenheath, Suffolk (temporarily detached to RAF Sculthorpe, Norfolk).

FB-111A 340th Bomb Group, Carswell AFB, Fort Worth, Texas; 4007th Combat Crew Training Sqn, Carswell; 4201st Test Sqn, Eglin AFB, Fort Walton Beach, Florida (SRAM test); today serving with 380th BW, Plattsburgh AFB, Plattsburgh, NY, and 509th BW, Pease AFB, Portsmouth, New Hampshire.

EF-111A 366th TFW, Mountain Home; today serving with 388th ECS (Electronic Combat Sqn), Mountain Home, which is training crews for other ECSs including one to be formed at RAF Upper Heyford.

Inventory

Numbers built, and in USAF/RAAF inventory, December 1982:

Model	Built	12/82
F-111A	159	105
F-111B	7	0
F-111C	24	20
F-111D	96	84
F-111E	94	81
F-111F	106	92
FB-111A	76	63
Total	562	445

Picture credits

PRINTED IN BELGIUM BY **Proost** INTERNATIONAL BOOK PRODUCTION